Paul's 1

Compact Edition

THE WRITINGS OF PAUL

Table of Contents

1 Corinthians 4

2 Corinthians 16

Colossians 26

Ephesians 41

Galatians 46

Hard Sayings of Paul 97

Hebrews 98

Covenant Forever 104

Paul-Anti-law? 105

Philippians 109

Romans 117

Walking in the Spirit 143

End-of-the-Law 151

Paul 161

Good-News 173

1 Thessalonians 178

2 Thessalonians 179

1 Timothy 181

2 Timothy 185

Introduction

Hello, peace and blessings to all. This book is intended to provide guidance and understanding concerning Paul's letters. Today's understanding of Paul's letters have been a debate for many centuries and the basis for many who believe that Paul taught that the Law or Torah had been done away with, and that "Grace" has replaced the Law. I pray as we look into key quotes of Paul, that we keep an open mind as to what is being said in context, and not attempt to Isogete. So many times we read the scriptures and writings with preconceptions which cause us to put our thoughts in the Word, and not letting the Word(s) define or rather interpret itself.

The Hebrew that is being utilized in this book is not according to a modern Hebrew traditional grammar. I opted to use the Paleo Hebrew transliterated sounds into the English language for the Fathers name and the Messiah's name.

This book will be utilizing words such as "Elohim (Instead of Alahiym (Paleo/ancient)) Glory (Instead of Esteem), Jews (Instead of Yahudiym), Holy (Instead of Set-apart or Qadesh/Qadash etc.), just to name a few. This is to help new readers trying to understand the message of this book. Sometimes people that are just coming out of a religion or belief that has no Hebraic knowledge would or could be confused and frustrated when trying to learn this Hebraic walk. This book may fall into many denominational groups that are not familiar with Hebrew words. I do not want Hebrew words to be a stumbling block for those that are new to this faith and walk.

Those that already are familiar with Hebrew, there will be a more Hebraic version.

One of the things I like to stress before reading any material concerning how we should believe is to pray first. Ask the Most High to open your ears and heart so that it will be received as He intends. I have incorporated the Apocrypha for added support.

1st CORINTHIANS

In all Paul's epistles, as in all the Scripture, a spirit of candor, humility, prayer, and industry is required. The knowledge of Elohim's (Mighty one(s)/God) truth is to be acquired only by toil, and candid investigation. The mind that is filled with prejudice is rarely enlightened. A proud or arrogant spirit seldom receives benefit from reading the Scripture, or any other book. Rather, one acquires the most complete, profound knowledge of the doctrines of Paul, and of the Book of Elohim (Mighty one(s)/God) in general, when one comes to the work of interpretation with the most humble heart; and the deepest sense of his dependence on the aid of the Spirit who in fact inspired Scripture. For "the meek will he guide in judgment, and the meek will he teach his way," *Psa. 25:9.*

CHAPTER 1

1Co. 1:10 Now I exhort you, brothers, through the name of our Sovereign Yahusha (replaced with Yeshua/Jesus) Messiah that you all say the same thing, and there be no divisions among you, but you be united in the same mind and in the same judgment.
- Pro 6:16 These six *things* Yahuah (Replaced with Lord/God) hates; yea, seven *are* an abomination unto Him
  Pro 6:17 a proud look, a lying tongue, and hands that shed innocent blood,
  Pro 6:18 a heart that plots evil plans, feet hurrying to run to mischief,
  Pro 6:19 a false witness who breathes lies, and **he who causes strife among brothers.**

1Co. 1:19 For it has been written, "I will destroy the wisdom of the wise, and I will set aside the understanding of the understanding ones." [See Isaiah 29:14].

1Co. 1:20 Where *is the* wise? Where *the* scribe? Where *the* lawyer of this world? Did Elohim (Mighty one(s)/God) not make the wisdom of this world foolish?
- NOBODY KNOWS IT ALL, SO WE SHOULD NOT SEPARATE FROM ONE ANOTHER BECAUSE WE DON'T AGREE ON EVERYTHING

CHAPTER 2

Milk

Paul taught that we should not stand in the wisdom of men, but Elohim, who has given us His Spirit to teach us His wisdom and to learn, perceive, understand and empower us to live out spiritual things. Paul preached Yahusha ^(replaced with Yeshua/Jesus) **alone to those that are immature or on** milk**. But deeper things such as the Law that was made Flesh among the mature.**

1Co. 2:2 For I decided not to know anything among you except Yahusha ^(replaced with Yeshua/Jesus) Messiah, and Him having been crucified.
1Co. 2:3 And I was with you in weakness, and in fear, and in much trembling.
1Co. 2:4 And my word and my preaching *was* not in enticing words of human wisdom, but in proof of *the* Spirit and of power,
1Co. 2:5 that your faith might not be in *the* wisdom of men, but in *the* power of Elohim ^{(Mighty one(s)/God)}.
1Co. 2:6 But we speak wisdom among the perfect, but not the wisdom of this age, nor of the rulers of this age, those being brought to nothing.
1Co 2:7 But we speak *the* wisdom of Elohim ^{(Mighty one(s)/God)} in a mystery, having been hidden, which Elohim ^{(Mighty one(s)/God)} predetermined before the ages for our glory,

1Cor. 3:1 And I, brethren, could not speak unto you as unto spiritual, but as unto carnal, *even* as unto babes in Messiah.
1Cor. 3:2 I have fed you with milk, and not with meat: for hitherto you were not able *to bear it*, neither yet now are you able.

1Pet. 2:1 Wherefore laying aside all malice, and all guile, and hypocrisies, and envies, and all evil speaking,
1Pet. 2:2 As newborn babes, desire the sincere milk of the word, that you may grow thereby;

Heb. 5:12 For when for the time you ought to be teachers, you have need that one teach you again which *be* the first principles of the oracles of Elohim ^{(Mighty one(s)/God)}; and are become such as have need of milk, and not of strong meat.

Heb. 5:13 For every one that uses milk *is* unskillful in the word of righteousness: for he is a babe.

Heb. 5:14 But strong meat belongs to them that are of full age, *even* those who by reason of use have their senses exercised to discern both good and evil.

Heb. 6:1 Therefore leaving the principles of the doctrine of Messiah, let us go on unto perfection; not laying again the foundation of repentance from dead works, and of faith toward Elohim ^{(Mighty one(s)/God)},

Heb. 6:2 Of the doctrine of baptisms, and of laying on of hands, and of resurrection of the dead, and of eternal judgment.

Heb. 6:3 And this will we do, if Elohim ^{(Mighty one(s)/God)} permit.

Milk according to Hebrews is understood as:

1. Knowing repentance form dead works
2. Faith towards Elohim ^{(Mighty one(s)/God)}
3. Doctrine of baptisms
4. Laying on of hands
5. Resurrection of the dead
6. Eternal judgment

Theses are teachings that one should know and understand, to have a fundamental foundation. Once one has these principles we are to move on to perfection. What is perfection? To find this answer we need to see what makes one perfect.

- 1Kings 8:61 Let your heart therefore be perfect with Yahuah ^(Replaced with Lord/God) our Elohim ^{(Mighty one(s)/God)}, to walk in his statutes, and to keep his commandments, as at this day.

CHAPTER 3

Unity is a sign of the Spirit; Denominations, Factions, Religion, and Divisions, are a sign of the Flesh. They were instituted by Man. The Messiah never called us into any religion or denomination. When we do this, it creates separation from a body that is to be one. We are to be One body in Messiah.

1Co. 3:3 For you are yet fleshy For where among you *is* jealousy, and strife, and division's are you not fleshly and walk according to man?
1Co. 3:4 For when one may say, Truly I am of Paul, and another, I of Apollos; are you not fleshly?
1Co. 3:21 So let no one glory in men; for all things are yours,
1Co. 3:22 whether Paul, or Apollos, or Cephas, or *the* world, or life, or death, or things present, or things to come; all are yours,
1Co. 3:23 and you are Messiah's, and Messiah *is* Elohim ^{(Mighty one(s)/God)}.

If we are Messiah's then we are Abraham's seed. The unity we already have is being in the family of Israel, one in the Messiah.

Gal. 3:26 for you are all sons of Elohim ^{(Mighty one(s)/God)} through faith in Messiah Yahusha ^(replaced with Yeshua/Jesus).
Gal. 3:27 For as many as were immersed into Messiah, you put on Messiah.
Gal. 3:28 There cannot be Jew nor Greek, there is no slave nor free-man, there is no male and female; for you are all one in Messiah Yahusha ^(replaced with Yeshua/Jesus).
Gal. 3:29 And if you *are* of Messiah, then you are a seed of Abraham, even heirs according to promise.

Joh. 17:10 And all My things are Yours, and Yours *are* Mine; and I have been esteemed in them.
Joh. 17:11 And no longer am I in the world, yet these are in the world; and I come to you. Holy Father, keep them in Your name, those whom You gave to Me, that *they* may be one as We *are*.

Joh. 17:20 And I do not pray concerning these only, but also concerning those who will believe in Me through their word;
Joh. 17:21 that all may be one, as You *are* in Me, Father, and I in You, that they also may be one in Us, that the world may believe that You sent Me.
Joh. 17:22 And I have given them the glory, which You have given Me, that they may be one, as We are One:
Joh. 17:23 I in them, and You in Me, that they may be perfected in one; and that the world may know that You sent Me and loved them,

even as You loved Me.

CHAPTER 5

Paul was still teaching that we should keep the Feast of Yahuah
(Replaced with Lord/God)

1Co 5:8 So let us keep *the* feast, not with old leaven, nor with leaven of malice and of evil, but with unleavened *bread* of sincerity and truth

CHAPTER 6

1Co. 6:12 All things are lawful to me, but not all things expedient. All things are lawful to me, but I will not be ruled by any.
1Co. 6:13 Foods for the belly, and the belly for foods, but Elohim ^{(Mighty one(s)/God)} will destroy both this and these. But the body *is* not for fornication, but for Yahuah ^(Replaced with Lord/God), and Yahuah ^(Replaced with Lord/God) for the body.

CHAPTER 7

1Co. 7:18 *Was* anyone called having been circumcised? Do not be uncircumcised. Was anyone called in un-circumcision? Do not be circumcised.
1Co. 7:19 Circumcision is nothing, and un-circumcision is nothing, but the keeping of Elohim ^{(Mighty one(s)/God)} commands.
- Paul is saying circumcision does not save, it is an Acts of obedience and not SALVATION.

Lamsa translation of Aramaic Peshitta
If a man was circumcised when he was called, let him not adhere to the party of un-circumcision. And if he was uncircumcised, when he was called, let him not be circumcised. For circumcision is nothing, and un-circumcision is nothing, but the keeping of Yahuah's ^(Replaced with Lord/God) commandments is everything.

Gal. 5:1 Then stand firm in the freedom with which Messiah made us free and do not be held again with a yoke of slavery.
Gal. 5:2 Behold, I Paul say to you that if you are circumcised, Messiah

will profit you nothing.

Gal. 5:3 And I witness again to every man being circumcised, that he is a debtor to do all the Law,

Gal. 5:4 *you* whoever are **justified by Law**, you were severed from Messiah; you fell from favor.

John Gill's Commentary

This is directly contrary to the notions of the Jews, who think they shall be saved for their circumcision, and that that will secure them from hell; they say no circumcised person goes down to hell, and that whoever is circumcised shall inherit the land; but there is none shall inherit the land, save a righteous person;

but everyone that is circumcised is called a righteous man; so that circumcision is their righteousness, on account of which they expect heaven and happiness.

Shemot Rabba, sect. 19. fol. 104. 4. Zohar in Exod. fol. 10. 2.

1Co. 7:19 Circumcision is nothing, and un-circumcision is nothing, but the keeping of Elohim's ^{(Mighty one(s)/God)} commands.

Why was Paul so adamant about circumcision? Because the Jews of his time almost worshipped the Act of circumcision more than Elohim ^{(Mighty one(s)/God)} "says R. Eliezar ben Azariah," un-circumcision is rejected, because by it the wicked are defiled, as it is said, "for all the Gentiles are uncircumcised"; says R. Ishmael, מילה גדולה, "great is circumcision"; for on account of it, thirteen covenants were made; says R. Jose, "great is circumcision", for it drives away the Sabbath, the weighty (command in the law, that is, it is obliged to give way to it); R. Joshua ben Korcha says, "great is circumcision", for it was not suspended to Moses the righteous one full hour; R. Nehemiah says, "great is circumcision", for it drives away plagues; says Rabba, "great is circumcision", for notwithstanding all the commands which Abraham our father did, he was not called perfect until he was circumcised; as it is said, "walk before me, and be you perfect"; says another, "great is circumcision", for had it not been for that, the Holy blessed Elohim ^{(Mighty one(s)/God)} would not have created his world; as it is said, "thus says Yahuah ^(Replaced with Lord/God), if my covenant be not with day and night, and if I have not appointed the ordinances of heaven and earth", "The Holy blessed Elohim ^{(Mighty one(s)/God)} (say they) rejects the uncircumcised, and brings them down to hell; as it is said,

- Ezek. 32:18, "son of man, wail for the multitude of Egypt, and cast them down";
- Isa. 5:14 "therefore hell has enlarged herself and opened her mouth", חק לבלי; that is, to him that has not the law of circumcision; as it is said, *Psa. 105:10* "and confirmed the same unto Jacob for a law, and to Israel for an everlasting covenant"; for no circumcised persons go down to hell:"

In Shabbat 137b it is stated that Circumcision is what keeps the universe going Blessed are You, O Sovereign, Who makes the covenant. 'He who circumcises slaves recites:'… Who has set-apart us with your commandments and has commanded us concerning circumcision. While he who pronounces the benediction recites: '… **Who has set-apart us with your commandments and has commanded us to cause the drops of the blood of the covenant to flow from them, since but for the blood of the covenant the ordinances of heaven and earth would not endure,** as it is said, If not my covenant by day and by night, I had not appointed the ordinances of heaven and earth. Blessed are You, O Sovereign, Who makes the covenant.'

CHAPTER 8

1Co. 8:4 Then concerning the eating of things sacrificed to idols, we know that an idol *is* nothing in *the* world, and that *there* is no other Elohim [(Mighty one(s)/God)] except one.

1Co. 8:5 For even if *some* are called gods, either in *the* heavens or on the earth; (even as there are many gods, and many sovereign's [(lord's/master's)]);

1Co. 8:6 but to us *there is* one Elohim [(Mighty one(s)/God)], the Father, of whom *are* all things, and we for Him, and one Sovereign Yahusha [(replaced with Yeshua/Jesus)] Messiah, through whom are all things, and we by Him.

1Co. 8:7 But the knowledge *is* not in all; but some being aware of the idol eat as an idolatrous sacrifice until now; and their conscience being weak is defiled.

1Co. 8:8 But food will not commend us to Elohim [(Mighty one(s)/God)]. For neither if we eat do we excel, nor if we do not eat are we lacking.

1Co. 8:9 But be careful lest this authority of yours become a cause of stumbling to the weak ones.

1Co. 8:10 For if anyone sees you, the *one* having knowledge, sitting in an idol-temple, will not the weak one's conscience be lifted up so as to eat things sacrificed to idols?

1Co 8:11 And on your knowledge the weak brother will fall, *he* for whom Messiah died.

1Co. 8:12 And sinning in this way against *your* brothers, and wounding their conscience, being weak, you sin against Messiah.

1Co. 8:13 On account of this, if food offends my brother, I will not at all eat flesh forever, so that I do not offend my brother.

CHAPTER 9

1Co. 9:20 And I became as a Jew to the Jews that I might gain Jews; to those under Law as under Law, that I might gain those under Law; 1Co. 9:21 to those without Law as without Law (not being without Law of Elohim ^{(Mighty one(s)/God)}, but under *the* law of Messiah), that I might gain *those* without Law.

Isa. 42:4 He shall not fail nor be crushed until He has set justice in the earth; and the coasts shall wait for His Law.

Is Messiah's Law Different than the Law given at Mount Sinai?

Isa. 42:21 Yahuah ^(Replaced with Lord/God) is delighted for His righteousness' sake; He will magnify the Law and make *it* honorable.

Joh. 7:16 Yahusha ^(replaced with Yeshua/Jesus) answered them and said, My doctrine is not Mine, but of the *One* who sent Me.

John 12:49 For I have not spoken of myself; but the Father which sent me, he gave me a commandment, what I should say, and what I should speak.

John 12:50 And I know that his commandment is life everlasting: whatsoever I speak therefore, even as the Father said unto me, so I speak.

The Messiah would never teach something that was different than what was given back in Mount Sinai. He was the one who was at

11

CHAPTER 10

1Co. 10:1 And I do not want you to be ignorant **brothers that** our fathers were all under the cloud, and all passed through the Sea.

The Corinthians were "Gentiles" yet their Fathers were under the cloud and pass through the sea. These are some clues as to who the Gentiles are.

1Co. 10:7 Neither be idolaters, even as some of them, as it has been written, "The people sat down to eat and drink, and stood up to play." *Ex. 32:6*

The golden calf incident at Mount Sinai, even though it was done to honor Elohim ^{(Mighty one(s)/God)} **it was and is still defined as Idolatry.**

- **Ex. 32:4** And he took *them* from their hand and formed it with an engraving tool. And he made it a casted calf. And they said, These *are* your gods, O Israel, who made you go up from the land of Egypt.
Ex. 32:5 And Aaron saw, and he built an altar before it. And Aaron called and said, A feast to Yahuah ^(Replaced with Lord/God) tomorrow.
Ex. 32:6 And they rose early on the morrow, and they offered burnt offerings and brought near peace offerings. And the people sat down to eat and drink, and rose up to play.

1Co. 10:11 And all these things happened to those *as* examples, and *it* was written for our warning, on whom the ends of the ages have come.

1Co. 10:18 Look at Israel according to flesh; are not those eating the sacrifices partakers of the altar?
1Co. 10:19 What then do I say, that an idol is anything, or that an idolatrous sacrifice is anything?
1Co. 10:20 But the things the nations sacrifice, "*they* sacrifice to demon's and not to Elohim ^{(Mighty one(s)/God)}." *Deut. 32:17* But I do not

want you to become sharers of demons;

1Co. 10:21 you cannot drink *the* cup of Yahuah ^(Replaced with Lord/God) and a cup of demons; you cannot partake of the table of Yahuah ^(Replaced with Lord/God), and a table of demons.

1Co. 10:22 Or do we provoke Yahuah ^(Replaced with Lord/God) to jealousy? Are we stronger than He? *Deut. 32:21*

1Co. 10:23 All things are lawful to me, but not all things expedient. All things are lawful to me, but not all things build up.

1Co. 10:24 Let no one seek the things of himself, but each one that of the other.

1Co. 10:25 Eat everything being sold in a meat market, examining nothing because of conscience,

1Co. 10:26 for "the earth *is* Yahuah's ^(Replaced with Lord/God), and the fullness of it." *Psa. 24:1*

- Rom 14:14 I know and am persuaded in Yahuah ^(Replaced with Lord/God) Yahusha ^(replaced with Yeshua/Jesus) that nothing by itself is common; except to the *one* deeming anything to be common, *it is* common.

1Co. 10:27 And if any of the unbelievers invite you, and you desire to go, eat everything set before you, examining nothing because of conscience.

1Co 10:28 But if anyone tells you, This is slain in sacrifice to idol's do not eat because of that one pointing *it* out and the conscience; for "the earth *is* Yahuah's ^(Replaced with Lord/God), and the fullness of it." *Psa. 24:1*

1Co. 10:29 But I say conscience, not that of himself, but that of the other. For why is my freedom judged by another's conscience?

1Co. 10:30 But if I partake by favor, why am I evil spoken of because of that *for* which I give thanks?

1Co. 10:31 Then whether you eat or drink, or whatever you do, do all things to the glory of Elohim ^{(Mighty one(s)/God)}

1Co. 10:32 Be without offense both to Jews and Greeks, & to the assembly of Elohim ^{(Mighty one(s)/God)}.

CHAPTER 11

1Co. 11:2 But I praise you, brothers, that in all things you have remembered me, and even as I delivered *them* to you, you hold fast the doctrines (TRADITIONS).

CHAPTER 12

Not being considered Gentiles anymore

1Co. 12:2 You know that being **led away**, you nations were led to voiceless idols

- **Eph. 2:11** Because of this, remember that you, the nations, *were* then in *the* flesh (those having been called Un-circumcision by those having been called Circumcision in the flesh made by hands)

- **Eph 4:17** Therefore, I say this, and witness in Yahuah ^(Replaced with Lord/God), that you no longer walk even as also the rest *of the* nations walk, in *the* vanity of their mind,

- **1Pe. 4:3** For *the* time of life having passed is sufficient for us to have worked out the will of the nations, having gone on in lasciviousness, lusts, drunkenness, parties, reveling, and lawless idolatries;

- **1Th. 4:5** not in passion of lust, even as also the nations *do*, not knowing Elohim ^{(Mighty one(s)/God)};

CHAPTER 14

1Co. 14:34 Let your women be silent in the assemblies, for it is not allowed to them to speak, but to be in subjection, as also the Law says. 1Co. 14:35 But if they desire to learn anything, let them question their husbands at home; for it is a shame for a woman to speak in an assembly.

John Gill's Commentary

for it is not permitted unto them to speak; that is, in public assemblies, in the church of Elohim ^{(Mighty one(s)/God)}, they might not speak with tongues, nor prophesy, or preach, or teach the word. All speaking is not prohibited; they might speak their experiences to the church, or give an account of the work of Elohim ^{(Mighty one(s)/God)} upon their souls; they might speak to one another in psalms, hymns, and spiritual songs;

or speak as an evidence in any case at a church meeting; but not in such sort, as carried in it direction, instruction, government, and authority. It was not allowed by Elohim ^{(Mighty one(s)/God)} that they should speak in any authoritative manner in the church; nor was it suffered in the churches of Messiah; nor was it admitted of in the Hebrew synagogue; there, we are told, the men came to teach, and the women לשמוע, "to hear": and one of their canons runs thus" a woman may not read (that is, in the law), בצבור, "in the congregation", or church, because of the honor of the congregation;" for they thought it a dishonorable thing to a public assembly for a woman to read, though they even allowed a child to do it that was capable of it. But they are commanded to be under obedience, as also says the law. In Gen. 3:16, "your desire shall be to your husband, and he shall rule over you". By this the apostle would signify, that the reason why women are not to speak in the church, or to preach and teach publicly, or be concerned in the ministerial function, is, because this is an Acts of power, and authority; of rule and government, and so contrary to that subjection which Elohim ^{(Mighty one(s)/God)} in his law requires of women unto men. The extraordinary instances of Deborah, Huldah, and Anna, must not be drawn into a rule or example in such cases. (T. Hieros Chagiga, fol. 75. 4. & T. Bab. Chagiga, fol. 3. 1. Maimon. Hilch. Tephilla, c. 12. sect. 17. T. Bab. Megilla, fol. 23. 1.

1Ti. 2:12 - But I suffer not a woman to teach, nor to usurp authority over the man, but to be in silence.

The first argument why it is not lawful for women to teach in the congregation? This is a position of authority, and would place them above men, for they would be their sovereigns: and this is against Elohim(s) ^{(Mighty one(s)/God)} ordinance.

These were issues faced during the time of the disciples. We believe if the Father has a message to give to His people, and uses a woman, this would still be a blessing. The Father pours His spirit out on all flesh.

2 CORINTHIANS

CHAPTER 3

2Co. 3:6 who also made us able ministers of a new covenant, not of letter, but of Spirit. For the letter kills, but the Spirit makes alive.

- **Rom. 7:6** But now we have been set free from the Law, having died *to that* in which we were held, so as *for* us to **serve in newness of spirit, and not** *in* **oldness of letter**.
  Rom 7:7 What shall we say then? *Is* the Law sin? Let it not be! But I did not know sin except through Law; for also I did not know lust except the Law said, "You shall not lust."

- **Rom. 8:2** For the Law of the Spirit of life in Messiah Yahusha [(replaced with Yeshua/Jesus)] set me free from the law of sin and of death.

- **Joh. 6:63** It is the Spirit that gives life. The flesh does not profit, nothing! **The Words which I speak to you are spirit and are life.**

John Gill's commentary
Gives life; it is a means in the hand of the Spirit of Elohim [(Mighty one(s)/God)], of quickening dead sinners, of healing the deadly wounds of sin, of showing the way of life by Messiah and of working faith in the soul, to look to him, and live upon him; it affords food for the support of the spiritual life, and revives souls under the most drooping circumstances. **The apostle may allude to a distinction among the Jews, between the body and soul of the law; the words, they say, are** גופא תורה, "the body of the law"; and the book of the law is the clothing; and besides these, there is דאוריתא נשמתא, "the soul of the law"; which wise men look

Is the Law Not Spiritual?

2Ti. 3:16 All **Scripture** *is* Elohim [(Mighty one(s)/God)]-breathed and profitable for doctrine, for reproof, for correction, for instruction in righteousness,

- **G2315**

  θεο¹νευστος

  theopneustos

  Thayer Definition:
  1) inspired by Elohim [(Mighty one(s)/God)], (1a) the contents of the scriptures
  Part of Speech: adjective
  A Related Word by Thayer's/Strong's Number: from G2316 and a presumed derivative of G4154

    G2316

    θεος

    theos

    Thayer Definition:
    1) a god or goddess, a general name of deities or divinities

      G4154

      ¹νεω

      pneo

      Thayer Definition:
      1) to breath, to blow
      1a) of the wind
      The word for spirit is:

        G4151

        ¹νευμα

        pneuma

A Related Word by Thayer's/Strong's Number: from G4154

Paul also said to the Romans that the Law is spiritual, so the letter spoken about in 2 Corinthians 3 cannot be the Law. Paul is comparing walking in the flesh versus walking in the Spirit. Verses 1-5 explains the context of what follows. Paul is teaching us not to trust in the letter of the law or our righteousness or pieces of paper that tell others what college courses we went through. Paul is telling us to walk in the Spirit where the Law is written in our hearts and we follow the Spirit of the Law.

- **Rom. 7:12** So indeed the Law *is* Holy, and the commandment

Holy and just and good.

- **Rom. 7:14** For we know that the Law is spiritual, but I am fleshly, having been sold under sin.

2Co. 3:1 Do we begin again to commend ourselves? Or do we, as some, need commendatory letters to you, or commendatory *ones* from you?

2Co. 3:2 You are our letter, having been inscribed in our hearts, being known and being read by all men,

2Co. 3:3 *it* having been made plain that you are Messiah's letter, served by us, not having been inscribed by ink, but by *the* Spirit of *the* living Elohim ^{(Mighty one(s)/God)}, not in tablets of stone, but in fleshly tablets of *the* heart.

2Co. 3:4 And we have such confidence through Messiah toward Elohim ^{(Mighty one(s)/God)};

2Co. 3:5 not that we are sufficient of ourselves to reason out anything as *being* out of ourselves, but our sufficiency *is* of Elohim ^{(Mighty one(s)/God)}

- In **Romans 2:28-29**, Paul is speaking about those who only have the outward physical sign (in Hebrew) of the covenant, which is brit milah or circumcision. But, because their lives are characterized by disobedience to the Law, they do not possess genuine belief (faith).

Paul vs. Moses

This same context is to be found in **2 Corinthians chapter 3** where Paul is
contrasting the ministry of Moses with his own. He says that the ministry of Moses brought death, while his [Paul's] brought life! Did Moses have bad material in the Law and Paul better material in the "Good News"? WRONG!

Rather, it was the hardened hearts and the stopped ears of the Israelite people that rendered Moses ministry one of death. Paul then expounds that when the Spirit takes away the hardness of heart and opens the ears of the deaf, the very message (the Law that Moses preached and taught to Israel (GIVES LIFE TO THE HEARER! You have to remember the only Scriptures that were around during Paul's ministry were the "Old Testament". When the work of the Spirit (the taking away of the veil) is manifested in a person's life, then the glory of the Messiah shines forth bringing the hearer belief and salvation!

The Curse of death

Rom. 5:12 Because of this, even as sin entered the world through one man, and death through sin, so also death passed to all men, inasmuch as all sinned.

Rom. 5:13 For sin was in *the* world until Law, but sin is not charged *where* there is no law;

Rom. 5:14 but death reigned from Adam until Moses, even on those who had not sinned in the likeness of Adam's transgression, who is a type of the coming *One.*

Rom. 5:15 But the free gift *is* not also like the deviation. For if by the deviation of the one the many died, much more the favor of Elohim ^{(Mighty one(s)/God)}, and the gift in favor, which *is* of the one Man, Yahusha ^(replaced with Yeshua/Jesus) Messiah, did abound to the many.

Rom. 5:16 And the gift *is* not as by one having sinned; for indeed the judgment *was* of one to condemnation, but the free gift *is* of many trespasses to justification.

Rom. 5:17 For if by the deviation of the one death reigned through the one, much more those who are receiving the abundance of favor and the gift of righteousness shall rule in life by the One, Yahusha ^(replaced with Yeshua/Jesus) Messiah.

Rom. 5:18 So then, as through one deviation *it was* toward all men to condemnation, so also through one righteous Acts toward all men to justification of life.

Rom. 5:19 For as through the one man's disobedience the many were constituted sinners, so also through the obedience of the One the many shall be constituted righteous.

Rom. 5:20 But Law came in besides, that the deviation might abound. But where sin abounded, favor much more abounded,

Rom. 5:21 that as sin ruled in death, so also favor might rule through righteousness to everlasting life, through Yahusha ^(replaced with Yeshua/Jesus) Messiah our Sovereign.

Definition of Law Means Instructions

Gal. 3:21 Then is the Law against the promises of Elohim (Mighty one(s)/God)? Let it not be! For if a law had been given which had been able to make alive, indeed righteousness would have been out of Law.
Gal. 3:22 But the Scripture locked up all under sin, that the promise by faith of Yahusha (replaced with Yeshua/Jesus) Messiah might be given to the ones believing.
Gal. 3:23 But before the coming of faith, we were guarded under Law, having been locked up to the faith being about to be revealed.
Gal. 3:24 So that the Law has become a trainer of us *until* Messiah, that we might be justified by faith.
Gal. 3:25 But faith coming, we are no longer under a trainer;
Gal. 3:26 for you are all sons of Elohim (Mighty one(s)/God) through faith in Messiah Yahusha (replaced with Yeshua/Jesus).
Gal. 3:27 For as many as were baptized into Messiah, you put on Messiah.
Gal. 3:28 There cannot be Jew nor Greek, there is no slave nor free-man, there is no male and female; for you are all one in Messiah Yahusha (replaced with Yeshua/Jesus).
Gal. 3:29 And if you *are* of Messiah, then you are a seed of Abraham, even heirs according to promise.

- More on this when we get to the Galatians

Legalism (Keep in Mind the over all problem in the scriptures and letters is SIN)

Rom 3:19 But we know that whatever the Law says, it speaks to those within the Law, so that every mouth may be stopped, and all the world be under judgment to Elohim (Mighty one(s)/God).
Rom 3:20 Because by works of Law not one of all flesh will be justified before Him, for through Law *is* full knowledge of sin. *Psa. 143:2*
Rom. 3:21 But now a righteousness of Elohim (Mighty one(s)/God) has been revealed apart from Law, being witnessed by the Law and the Prophets,
Rom. 3:22 even the righteousness of Elohim (Mighty one(s)/God) through faith of Yahusha (replaced with Yeshua/Jesus) Messiah toward all and upon all those believing; for there is no difference,

Rom. 3:23 for all sinned and fall short of the glory of Elohim ^{(Mighty one(s)/God)},

Rom. 3:24 being justified freely by His favor through the redemption in Messiah Yahusha ^(replaced with Yeshua/Jesus),

Rom. 3:25 whom Elohim ^{(Mighty one(s)/God)} set forth *as* a propitiation through faith in His blood, as a demonstration of His righteousness through the passing over of the sins that had taken place before, in the forbearance of Elohim ^{(Mighty one(s)/God)},

Rom. 3:26 for a demonstration of His righteousness in the present time, for His being just and justifying the *one* that *is* of the faith of Yahusha ^(replaced with Yeshua/Jesus).

Rom. 3:27 Then where *is* the boasting? It was excluded. Through what law? Of works? No, but through a Law of faith.

Rom. 3:28 Then we conclude a man to be justified by faith without works of Law.

Rom. 3:29 Or *is He* the Elohim ^{(Mighty one(s)/God)} of Jews only, and not also of the nations? Yes, of the nations also,

Rom. 3:30 since *it is* one Elohim ^{(Mighty one(s)/God)} who will justify circumcision by faith, and un-circumcision through faith.

Rom. 3:31 Then *is* the Law **annulled** through faith? Let it not be! But we establish Law.

Rom. 7:10 And the commandment, which *was* to life, this was found *to be* death to me;

Rom 7:11 for sin taking occasion through the commandment deceived me, and through it killed *me*.

Rom. 7:12 So indeed the Law *is* Holy, and the commandment Holy and just and good.

Rom. 7:13 Then that *which is* good, *has it* become death to me? Let it not be! But sin, that it might appear *to be* sin, having worked out death to me through the good, in order that sin might become excessively sinful through the commandment.

Rom. 7:14 For we know that the Law is spiritual, but I am fleshly, having been sold under sin.

Does this mean the Law was to cease?

- **Psa. 111:7** The works of His hands *are* truth and all His commandments *are* true,

Psa. 111:8 standing firm forever and ever; *they are* done in truth and uprightness.

Ecc 12:13 Let us hear the conclusion of the whole matter: Fear Elohim [(Mighty one(s)/God)], and keep his commandments: for this *is* the whole *duty* of man.

Done away/abolished, is the same word translated as void in Romans 3 where Paul says the Law is not made void by faith, it is established

- **Rom. 3:31** Then *is* the Law annulled through faith? **Let it not be!** But we **establish Law**.

- **G2673** καταργεω *katargeo*
  Thayer Definition:
  1) to render idle, unemployed, inactivate, inoperative
  1a) to cause a person or thing to have no further efficiency
  1b) to deprive of force, influence, power
  2) to cause to cease, put an end to, do away with, annul, abolish
  2a) to cease, to pass away, be done away
  2b) to be severed from, separated from, discharged from, loosed from any one
  2c) to terminate all intercourse with one
  Part of Speech: verb
  A Related Word by Thayer's/Strong's Number: from G2596 and G691

So Shaul [(Paul)] *asks the question in Romans 3:31*

- ***"Do we make void the T[h]urah through faith?"***
  "Elohim [(Mighty one(s)/God)] forbid: yea, we **establish** the T[h]urah/law*."

- 2673. **katarge÷w katargeo**, *kat-arg-eh´-o;* from 2596 and 691; to be (render) entirely idle (useless), literally or figuratively: — abolish, cease, cumber, deliver, destroy, do away, become (make) of no (none, without) effect, fail, loose, bring (come) to nought, put away (down), vanish away, make void.

- 2476. **i°sthmi histemi**, *his´-tay-mee;* a prolonged form of a primary **sta¿w stao**; to stand (transitively or intransitively), used in various applications (literally or figuratively): — abide, appoint, bring, continue, covenant, establish, hold up.

22

- Because we are saved by favor through faith, we do not void the law. We still follow the T[h]urah.

So we establish the T[h]urah, once we are saved by favor [grace] through faith.

The glory of the Good News excels that of the Law

2Co. 3:8 how much rather the ministry of the Spirit will be in glory!
2Co. 3:9 For if the ministry of condemnation *was* glory, much rather the ministry of righteousness abounds in glory.
2Co. 3:10 For even that which has been made glorious has not been made magnified in this respect, because of the surpassing glory.
2Co. 3:11 For if the thing done away was through worship, much rather the thing remaining *is* in worship.

- **1391.** δόξα **doxa,** *dox´-ah;* from the base of 1380; glory (as very apparent), in a wide application (literal or figurative, objective or subjective): — dignity, glory(-ious), honour, praise, **worship.**

John Gill's commentary
Distinguish between the law as a covenant of works, and as a rule of walk and conversation; as a covenant of works it is done away, as a rule of walk and conversation it still continues: distinguish between persons and persons; to them that are redeemed from it, it is done away; to them that are under it, it remains; and lastly, distinguish between a right and a wrong use of it; **as to any use of it to justify us before Elohim** [Mighty one(s)/God]**, by our obedience to it, it is done away; but as it may be of use to convince Sinners of sin, and to direct saints in a course of righteousness, so it abides.**

The Good news is "that which remains"; which denotes the continued efficacy, the incorruptibleness, the inexpugnableness, and duration of it; notwithstanding all the opposition of men and devils to it, still its blessings, promises, doctrines,
ordinances, and effects continue; it remains in the Scriptures, in the church, in the hearts of believers, and in the world too, until all the

23

elect of Elohim ^{(Mighty one(s)/God)} are gathered in: now as things that remain are much more glorious than those which are done away, so the Good news must be much more glorious than the law.

2Co. 3:13 And not as "Moses, *who* put a veil over his face," for the sons of Israel not to gaze at the end of the *thing* being **done away.** *Ex. 34:35*

2Co 3:14 But their thoughts were hardened, for until the present *time* the same veil remains on the reading of the Old Covenant, not being unveiled, that it is being done away in Messiah.

2Co 3:15 But until today, when Moses is being read, a veil lies on their heart.

2Co 3:16 But whenever it turns to Yahuah ^(Replaced with Lord/God), the veil is taken away.

Ex. 34:34

2Co 3:17 And Yahuah ^(Replaced with Lord/God) *is* the Spirit; and where the Spirit of Yahuah ^(Replaced with Lord/God) *is*, there *is* freedom. *Jm. 1:22-25*

CHAPTER 5

2Co. 5:5 And the *One* having worked in us for this same thing *is* Elohim ^{(Mighty one(s)/God)}, who also *is* giving us the earnest of the Spirit.
- The Greek word for earnest is arrabon from the Hebrew word arabon from arab which is translated surety in *Psa.119:122*

CHAPTER 6

2Co. 6:14 Do not be unequally yoked *with* unbelievers. For what partnership does righteousness *have* with lawlessness? And what fellowship does light *have* with darkness?
- 458. ἀνομία **anomia,** *an-om-ee´-ah;* from 459; illegality, i.e. **violation of law or (genitive case) wickedness: — iniquity, x transgress(-ion of) the law, unrighteousness.**
- **By definition, UNRIGHTEOUSNESS IS VIOLATION OF THE LAW**

2Co. 6:15 And what agreement does Messiah *have* with Belial? Or what part does a believer *have* with an unbeliever?
- Doesn't sound like Paul thinks the law is not for believers.

24

- Take a look at the parallels in verses 14 and 15.
  Believers vs. Unbelievers.
  Righteousness vs. Unrighteousness (Which means lawless or
  violator of the law) Messiah vs. Belial (The lawless one).
  Light vs. Darkness. Match the color pattern.

2Co. 6:15 - And what concord has Messiah with Belial?....
The word "Belial" is a Hebrew word, and is only used in this place in
the New Testament, but often in the Old Testament; this word is
differently read and pronounced, some copies read it "Beliar", and
accordingly in the Ethiopic version it is "Belhor", and by Jerom read
Belvir; but he observes, that it is more rightly called Belial: in some
copies it is "Belias", and so Tertullian read it; and Jerom says, that
most corruptly read it "Belias", for "Belial": some derive it from בלי ,
"Beli", and עלה , "Elah", and signifies "without ascent"; one in a very
low condition, of low life, that never rises up, and comes to anything;
to which Kimchi's etymology of the word seems to agree, who says,
that Belial is a wicked man, יצליח ובל בליעלה , "who does not succeed,
and does not prosper": others say it signifies one that is עול בלי , "Beli
Ol, without a yoke", without the yoke of the law; so Jarchi explains
children of Belial, in *Deut. 13:13* without yoke, who break off the
yoke of Elohim ^{(Mighty one(s)/God)}; and so say the Talmudists, "children of
Belial, are children that break off שמים עול, "the yoke of heaven" (i.e.
the law) from their necks;"
Belial (βελιαρ) *Beliar. Belial* is a transcript of the Hebrew, meaning
worthlessness or *wickedness*. The Septuagint renders it variously by
transgressor, *impious*, *foolish*, *pest*. Belial is the antithesis of Messiah.
Messiah is the Lawgiver, while Belial is the lawless one.

2Th. 2:3 Do not let anyone deceive you in any way, because *that Day
will not come* unless first comes the falling away, and **the man of sin**
is revealed, the son of perdition,

2Th. 2:7 For **the mystery of lawlessness** already is working, only he
is holding back now, until it comes out of the midst.
2Th. 2:8 And **then "the Lawless One" will be revealed, "whom"**
"Yahuah ^(Replaced with Lord/God)" "will consume" "by the spirit of His**
mouth," and will bring to naught by the brightness of His presence.
Isa. 11:4

25

2 Corinthians 6:14-7:1= Yahuah's ^(Replaced with Lord/God) call to His believers throughout all time

Gen. 12:1 And Yahuah ^(Replaced with Lord/God) had said to Abram, Go out from your land and from your kindred, and from your father's house, to the land, which I will show you.
Gen. 12:2 And I will make of you a great nation. And I will bless you and make your name great; and you will be a blessing.
Gen. 12:3 And I will bless those who bless you, and curse the one despising you. And in you all families of the earth shall be blessed.

Gen 26:5 Because that Abraham obeyed my voice, and kept my charge, my commandments, my statutes, and my laws.
Ex. 19:5 And now if listening you will listen to My voice, and will keep My covenant, you shall become a special treasure to Me above all the nations, for all the earth *is* Mine.
Ex. 19:6 And you shall become a kingdom of priests for Me, a Holy nation. These *are* the words, which you shall speak to the sons of Israel.

Isa. 52:10 Yahuah ^(Replaced with Lord/God) has bared His Holy arm in the eyes of all the nations; and all the ends of the earth shall see the salvation of our Elohim ^{(Mighty one(s)/God)}.

Isa. 52:11 Turn! Turn! Go out from there! Touch not the unclean! Go out of her midst, purify yourselves, bearers of the vessels of Yahuah ^(Replaced with Lord/God).

Rev. 18:4 And I heard another voice out of Heaven saying, My people, come out of her, that you may not share in her **sins**, and that you may not receive of her plagues;

1 John 3:4 sin is transgression of the law

COLOSSIANS

CHAPTER 2

Col. 2:8 Watch that there not be one robbing you through philosophy and empty deceit, **according to** the tradition of men, **according to** the elements of the world, and not according to Messiah.

- **Gal. 4:3** So we also, when we were infants, we were **under the** elements of the world, **being enslaved.**

- **Gal. 4:9** But now, knowing Elohim [(Mighty one(s)/God)], but rather being known by Elohim [(Mighty one(s)/God)], how do **you turn again to the** weak and poor elements **to which you desire again to slave anew**?

- The weak and poor elements are the traditions of men, and the world. Not the law of Elohim [(Mighty one(s)/God)]

- **Hos. 4:6** My people are cut off for lack of knowledge. Because you rejected the knowledge, I also rejected you from being priest to Me. Since you have forgotten the Law of your Elohim [(Mighty one(s)/God)], I will forget your son's even. I Israel became slaves to the elements of the world and statutes and judgments that were not good for us.

Col. 2:9 For in Him dwells all the fullness of the Mightiness [(Divinity)] bodily;
Col. 2:10 and having been filled, you are in Him, who is the Head of all rule and authority
Col. 2:11 in whom also you were circumcised with a circumcision not made by hands, in the putting **off of the body of the sins** of the flesh, by the circumcision of Messiah,
Col. 2:12 being buried with Him in baptism, in whom also you were raised through the faith of the working of Elohim [(Mighty one(s)/God)], raising Him from among the dead.
Col. 2:13 And you, being dead in the **trespasses** [(Side step, deviation, Sin, transgression)] and the un-circumcision of your flesh, He made alive together with Him, having forgiven you all the **trespasses** [(Side step, deviation, Sin, transgression)],
Col. 2:14 blotting out the handwriting in the ordinances against us, which was contrary to us, even *He* has taken it out of the midst, nailing it to the cross;

Is the Law against us?

Deut. 6:24 And Yahuah ^(Replaced with Lord/God) commanded us to do all these statutes, to fear Yahuah ^(Replaced with Lord/God) our Elohim ^{(Mighty one(s)/God)}, for our good always, that he might preserve us alive, as *it is* at this day.

Prov. 3:1 My son, forget not my law; but let our heart keep my commandments

Prov. 6:23 For the commandment is a lamp and the law is light; and reproofs of instruction are a way of life

Prov 7:2 Keep my commandments and live; and my law as the apple of thine eye

HANDWRITING

- **G5498** χειρογραφον cheirographon *khi-rog'-raf-on*
  Neuter of a compound of G5495 and G1125; something *hand written* (*"chirograph"*), that is, a *manuscript* (specifically a legal *document* or *bond* (figuratively)): - handwriting.
  Thayer Definition:
  1) a handwriting, what one has written by his own hand?
  2) a note of hand or writing in which one acknowledges that money has either been deposited with him or lent to him by another, to be returned at the appointed time **The bond written in ordinances that was against us** (to kath' hemon cheirographon tois dogmasin). The late compound cheirographon (cheir, hand, grapho) is very common in the papyri for a **certificate of debt or bond**, many of the original cheirographa (handwriting, "chirography"). See Deissmann, *Scripture Studies*, p. 247.

The signature made a legal debt or bond as Paul says in *Phm. 1:18*.: "I Paul have written it with mine own hand, I will repay it."

- ORDINANCES
  G1378 δογμα dogma *dog'-mah*

28

The word "Ordinances" in the Greek is Dogma, which can refer to Civil Laws see *Acts 17:7*
Ordinances in (Col. 2:14) and Decrees (Luk. 2:1) This word never refers to the Law. From the base of G1380; a *law* (civil, ceremonial or ecclesiastical): - decree, ordinance.

Eph. 2:15 Having abolished in his flesh the enmity, *even* the law of commandments *contained* in ordinances; for to make in himself of twain one new man, *so* making peace;

Acts 17:7 whom Jason has received. And these all Acts contrary to the decrees of Caesar, saying there is another king, Yahusha ^(replaced with Yeshua/Jesus).

Luk. 2:1 And it happened in those days, a decree went out from Caesar Augustus *for* all the habitable world to be registered.
   • δογμα In the LXX

Dan. 2:13 And the decree went forth that the wise *men* should be slain; and they sought Daniel and his fellows to be slain.

Dan. 3:10 You, O king, has made a decree, that every man that shall hear the sound of the cornet, flute, harp, sackbut, psaltery, and dulcimer, and all kinds of music, shall fall down and worship the golden image:

Dan. 4:6 Therefore made I a decree to bring in all the wise *men* of Babylon before me, that they might make known unto me the interpretation of the dream.

Dan. 6:8 Now, O king, establish the decree, and sign the writing, that it be not changed, according to the law of the Medes and Persians, which alters not.
Dan 6:9 Wherefore king Darius signed the writing and the decree.
Dan 6:10 Now when Daniel knew that the writing was signed, he went into his house; and his windows being open in his chamber toward Jerusalem, he kneeled upon his knees three times a day, and prayed, and gave thanks before his Elohim ^{(Mighty one(s)/God)}, as he did aforetime.

- **These are** ordinances **of man**, which Paul speaks of in the end of the same chapter.

Col. 2:20 Wherefore if you be dead with Messiah from **the rudiments of the world, why, as though living in the world, are you subject to** ordinances,
Col. 2:21 (Touch not taste no; handle not
Col. 2:22 Which all are to perish with the using;) after the **commandments and doctrines of men**?

Debt book of sins

John Gill

This the Jews call חוב שטר, shetar chob "the writing of the debt/bill of debt", and is the very phrase the Syriac version uses here: now this was as a debt book, which showed and testified the debts of men; that is, their sins, how many they are guilty of, and what punishment is due unto them: Tzeror Hammor, fol. 87. 1, 3.
Num. 5:23 And the priest shall write these curses in a book, and shall blot *them* with the bitter waters.

Col. 2:14 blotted out the handwriting of our debts, which [handwriting] existed against us, and took [it] from the midst, and affixed [it] to his cross.

Matt. 6:12 and forgive us our debts as we also forgive our debtors.

Isa. 65:6 Behold, *it is* **written before me**: I will not keep silence, but will recompense, even recompense into their bosom,

Rev. 20:12 And I saw the dead, small and great, stand before Elohim ^{(Mighty one(s)/God)}; and the books were opened: and another book was opened, which is of life: and the dead were judged out of those things which were written in the books, according to their works.

This doctrine of the debt book of sins is found in 1st century apocryphal literature as well

Enoch 98:6-7

I have sworn unto you, **you sinners,** by the Holy Great One, that all **your evil deeds are revealed in the heavens**, and that none of your deeds of oppression are covered and hidden. And do not think in your spirit nor say in your heart that you do not know and that you do not see that **every sin is every day recorded in heaven in the presence of the Most High**. From henceforth you know that all your oppression wherewith you oppress is **written down every day till the day of your judgment**.

Jubilees Chapter 5

13 righteous each in his kind always. And the judgment of all is ordained and **written on the heavenly** tablets in righteousness -even (the judgment of) all who depart from the path which is ordained for them to walk in; and if they walk not therein, **judgment is written down for every creature and for every kind.**
14 And there is nothing in heaven or on earth, or in light or in darkness, or in Sheol or in the depth, or in the place of darkness (which is not judged); and all their judgments are
15 **ordained and written and engraved**.

The interpretation of "Debt Book of sins" is confirmed in the Aramaic reading of Colossians 2:14

Etheridge

Colossians 2:14 and has blotted out in his mandates the writing of our debts that was against us, and has taken it from the midst, and affixed it to his stake;

Murdock

Colossians 2:14 and, by his mandates, he blotted out the handwriting of our debts, which [handwriting] existed against us, and took [it] from the midst, and affixed [it] to his stake.

Lamsa
Col. 2:14 And by his commandments he cancelled the written bond of our sins, which stood against us; and he took it out of the way, nailing it to his stake;

- The word for commandments is the Hebrew equivalent of **pequdah**, in the Aramaic the phrase is b'fuqdunahe. B' (in, at, with, by) his **pequdot**.

The word for handwriting is **shatar**
The word for debts in the Aramaic is **Chabbanen** the equivalent of **Chob**

The Hebrew equivalent of the Aramaic phrase **shatar chabbanen** is **shatar chob** spoken of by Tzeror Hammor

Looking at the Greek text agrees with the Aramaic

having blotted out the handwriting that was against us in/by the decrees (tois dogmasin)

Col 2:14 εξαλειψας G1813 (G5660)[HAVING BLOTTED OUT] το G3588[THE] καθ G2596[AGAINST] ημων G2257[US] χειρογραφον G5498[HANDWRITING] τοις G3588[IN THE] δογμασιν G1378[DECREES,] ο G3739[WHICH] ην G2258(G5713)[WAS] υ¹εναντιον G5227[ADVERSE] ημιν G2254[TO US,] και G2532[ALSO] αυτο G846[IT] ηρκεν G142(G5758)[HE HAS TAKEN] εκ G1537[OUT OF] του G3588[THE] μεσου G3319[MIDST,] ¹ροσηλωσας G4338(G5660)[HAVING NAILED] αυτο G846[IT] τω G3588[TO THE] σταυρω G4716[CROSS;]

So was the Law nailed to the cross?

1Pe. 2:24 who "Himself carried up in His body **our sins" onto the tree;** that dying to **sins**, we might live to righteousness, of whom "*by* His wound you were healed."

Rom. 7:7 What shall we say then? *Is the law sin?* **Elohim** (Mighty one(s)/God) **forbid**. Nay, I had not known sin, but by the law: for I had not known lust, except the law had said, You shall not covet.

Blotting out SINS

Psa. 51:1 *To the chief musician, A Psalm of David when Nathan the* *prophet came to him, after he had gone in to Bathsheba.* Show me favor, O Elohim ^{(Mighty one(s)/God)}, according to Your loving-kindness, according to the multitude of Your tender mercies; **blot out my transgressions**.

Psa. 51:9 Hide Your face from my sins, and **blot out all my iniquities.**
Psa. 51:10 Create in me a clean heart, O Elohim ^{(Mighty one(s)/God)}; and renew a steadfast spirit within me.

Isa 43:25 I, even I, *am* **He who blots out your trespasses for My sake**; and I will not remember your sins.

Isa. 44:22 I have blotted out your transgressions like a thick cloud; and your sins like a cloud. Return to Me, for I have redeemed you.

Acts 3:19 Therefore, repent, and convert, for **the blotting out of your sins,** so that times of refreshing may come from *the* face of Yahuah (Replaced with Lord/God) ,

1 John 3:4 Whosoever commits sin transgresses also the law; for sin is the transgression of the law.

Taking away the curse/SIN

Gal. 3:13 Messiah redeemed us from the curse of the Law, having become a curse for us; for it has been written, "Cursed *is* everyone having been hung on a tree;" *Deut. 21:23*

Gal. 3:21 Then is the Law against the promises of Elohim ^{(Mighty one(s)/God)}? Let it not be! For if a law had been given which had been able to make alive, indeed righteousness would have been out of Law.

Joh. 1:29 On the morrow, John sees Yahusha ^(replaced with Yeshua/Jesus) coming toward him and said, Behold! The Lamb of Elohim ^{(Mighty one(s)/God)}, **taking away** the sin
of the world!

Joh. 7:49 But this people who knows not the law are cursed.

Is Yahuah's ^(Replaced with Lord/God) Ordinances, Commandments and the Law against us?

Lev. 18:5 You shall therefore keep my statutes, and my judgments: which if a man do, he shall live in them: I *am* Yahuah ^(Replaced with Lord/God).

Deut. 10:13 to keep the commandments of Yahuah ^(Replaced with Lord/God), and His statutes which I am

Deut. 6:24 And Yahuah ^(Replaced with Lord/God) commanded us to do all these statutes, to fear Yahuah ^(Replaced with Lord/God) our Elohim ^{(Mighty one(s)/God)} for our good forever, to keep us alive, as today.
Deut. 6:25 And it shall be our righteousness, if we observe to do all these commandments before Yahuah ^(Replaced with Lord/God) our Elohim ^{(Mighty one(s)/God)}, as he has commanded us.

Deut. 5:29 Would that this heart of theirs *would be* like this always, to fear Me, and to keep all My commandments, that it might be well with them, and with their sons forever.

Prov. 28:9 He that turns away his ear from hearing the law, even his prayer *shall be* abomination. [Scriptures says He change not, *Mal. 3:6* For I *am* Yahuah ^(Replaced with Lord/God), I change not;].

Let's continue with the letter to the Colossians

Col. 2:15 having stripped the rulers and the authorities, He made a show of them in public, triumphing *over* them in it.

Messiah died to give us victory over our enemies; The Devil, Demons, Sin, and Death.
Law was never our enemy. If you break the Law (Like any Law), there were consequences. In Scripture these are what brings a curse. *Deut. 27:14-26*

But if you keep His commandments and Laws, they bring blessings.

- Also they bring long life as well. Would the Father do away with that?

The Law brings blessings and curses. What the Messiah did was absorbed our curses, and bore them on Himself and nailing them to the cross. IT WAS NOT THE LAW THAT WAS NAILED, BUT THE CURSES OF THE LAW.

Heb. 2:14 Since, then, the children have partaken of flesh and blood, in like manner He Himself also shared the same things, that through death He might cause to cease the *one* having the power of death, that is, the devil;
Heb. 2:15 and might set these free, as many as by fear of death were subject to slavery through all the *lifetime* to live.

1Joh. 3:8 The *one* **practicing sin is of the devil** [Sin is transgression of the law, see verse four], because the devil sins from *the* beginning.
 For this the Son of Elohim (Mighty one(s)/God) was revealed, that He might undo the works of the devil.
1Joh. 3:9 Everyone who has been begotten of Elohim (Mighty one(s)/God) does not sin, because His seed abides in him, and he is not able to sin, because he has been born of Elohim (Mighty one(s)/God).
1Joh. 3:10 By this the children of Elohim (Mighty one(s)/God) and the children of the devil are revealed: Everyone not practicing righteousness is not of Elohim (Mighty one(s)/God); also the *one* not loving his brother.

Psa 119:172 My tongue shall speak of your word: for all you commandments are righteousness

Is 51:7 Listen to me, you that know righteousness, the people in whose heart is my law; fear you not the reproach of men, neither you be afraid of their reviling
(see Deut 6:25[Righteousness is keeping His Laws and Commandments]) Discern.

Col. 2:16 Then do not let anyone judge you in eating, or in drinking, or in part of a feast, or of a new moon, or of Sabbaths,

Col. 2:17 which are a shadow of coming things, but the body *is* of Messiah.

- Heb. 10:1 For the Law had a shadow of the coming good things, not the image *itself* of *those* things. *Appearing* year by year with the same sacrifices, which they offer continually, they never are able to perfect the ones drawing near.

The Feast and Sabbath's are a shadow of thing TO COME. They are not here yet. So they are still binding. The Feast and Sabbath's Days point to three things
1. How to walk righteously, and how to treat one another, and how the Father wants to be treated Deut. *6:24-25; Isa. 51:7*
2. Points to the Messiah *Luke 24:43-45*
3. How to prepare for End Time Prophecies. *1 Thess. 5:1-5*

So since the Messiah has come all things are fulfilled, right?

- **Matt. 5:18** For verily I say unto you, Till heaven and earth pass, one jot or one tittle shall in no wise pass from the law, **till all be fulfilled**.

- **Matt. 26:29** But I say to you, I will not at all drink of this fruit of the vine after this until **that day when I drink it new with you in the kingdom of My Father**.

- **Rev.** 17:17 For Elohim ^{(Mighty one(s)/God)} has put in their hearts to fulfill his will, and to agree, and give their kingdom unto the beast, until the words of Elohim ^{(Mighty one(s)/God)} **shall be fulfilled**.

- **Rev.** 20:3 And cast him into the bottomless pit, and shut him up, and set a seal upon him, that he should deceive the nations no more, till the thousand years should **be fulfilled**: and after that he must be loosed a little season.

- All has not been fulfilled. So the Law still stands according to *Matt. 5:18*

Col. 2:20 If, then, you died with Messiah from the elements of the world, why are you under *its* decrees, as living in *the* world?

Col. 2:21 Do not handle, do not taste, do not touch,

Col. 2:22 which things are all for corruption in the using, according to the "injunctions and teachings of men." *Isa. 29:13*

Col. 2:23 Which things indeed *appear to be* a matter of having wisdom in self-imposed worship and humility, and severity *in abuse* of *the* body, *but are* not of any value with regards to gratification of the flesh.

- If Paul is calling the Law of the Most High an element of the world, and an injunction, and or teaching of men. He is a false prophet. See *Deut. 13:1-5*

The Aramaic translation of Colossians 2:20 gives the meaning: if we are dead to the world, why are we allowing ourselves to be judged by the world as if we were still a part of it? The meaning refers back to verse 16 where we are not to let the world judge us concerning Sabbaths etc. The world judges us because we DO the Law, the meaning of the text is not that we shouldn't do the Law but not let people judge us for doing it.

Elements of the world

- Gal. 4:3 So we also, when we were infants, we were under the elements of the world, being enslaved.

Commandments of men is never a reference to the Law

Isa. 29:13 And Yahuah ^(Replaced with Lord/God) says, Because this people draws near with its mouth, and they honor Me with its lip; but its heart is far from Me, and their fear of Me is taught *by* the commandments *of* men;

Matt. 15:2 Why do your disciples transgress the tradition of the elders? For they do not wash their hands when they eat bread.

Matt. 15:3 But answering He said to them, Why do you also transgress the command of Elohim ^{(Mighty one(s)/God)} on account of your tradition?

Matt. 15:4 For Elohim ^{(Mighty one(s)/God)} commanded, saying, "Honor your father & mother," *Ex. 20:12; Deut. 5:16* &
"The one speaking evil of father or mother, by death let him die." *Ex. 21:17*
Matt. 15:5 But you say, Whoever says to the father or the mother, A gift, whatever you would gain from me;
Matt. 15:6 and in no way he honors his father or his mother. And you annulled the command of Elohim ^{(Mighty one(s)/God)} on account of your tradition.
Matt. 15:7 Hypocrites! Well did Isaiah prophesy concerning you, saying:
Matt. 15:8 "This people draws near to Me with their mouth, and with *their* lips honor Me; but their heart holds far off from Me.
Matt. 15:9 But in vain they worship Me, teaching *as* doctrines *the* precepts of men."
Isa. 29:13

CHAPTER 3

Who are the Sons of disobedience?

Col. 3:6 on account of which things the wrath of Elohim ^{(Mighty one(s)/God)} is coming on the **sons of disobedience**,

Paul just named things that are contrary to the Law and mentions "Sons of disobedience". Could Paul merely not be talking about in chapter 2 that the Law is nailed to the cross and done away with? Let's see who are the sons of disobedience.

Eph. 2:2 in which you formerly walked according to the course of this world, according to the ruler of the authority of the air, the spirit now working in the **sons of disobedience**,

Eph. 5:6 Let no one deceive you with empty words, for through these *things* the wrath of Elohim ^{(Mighty one(s)/God)} comes on the **sons of disobedience**.

Isa. 30:8 Now go, write it before them in a table, and note it in a book, that it may be for the time to come for ever and ever:

Isa. 30:9 That this *is* a **rebellious people**, lying children, children *that* will not hear the law of Yahuah ^(Replaced with Lord/God):

Sir. 10:19 They that fear Yahuah ^(Replaced with Lord/God) are a sure seed, and they that love him an honorable plant: **they that regard not the law are a dishonorable seed; they that transgress the commandments are a deceivable seed**.

Col. 3:16 Let the Word of Messiah dwell in you richly, in all wisdom teaching and exhorting yourselves in psalms and hymns and spiritual songs, singing with favor in your hearts to Yahuah ^(Replaced with Lord/God).

- **2Ti. 3:15** and that **from a babe you know the Holy Scriptures**, those being able to make you wise to salvation through belief in Messiah Yahusha ^(replaced with Yeshua/Jesus). [What was/is Holy Scriptures during their time? The "Old testament"].
  2Ti. 3:16 **All Scripture** *is* Elohim ^{(Mighty one(s)/God)}-breathed and profitable for doctrine, for reproof, for correction, for instruction in righteousness,
- 2Ti. 3:17 so that the man of Elohim ^{(Mighty one(s)/God)} may be perfected, being fully furnished for every good work.

- **Deut. 18:19** And it shall be, whoever will not listen to My Words which he shall speak in My name, I will require it at his hand.

  The Scripture at that time was and as well as should still also be today is the TANAK or as is commonly called today, the "Old Testament."

He will judge the World by His faith/Word.

Psa. 96:13 Before Yahuah ^(Replaced with Lord/God): for he comes, for he comes to judge the earth: **he shall judge the world with righteousness, and the people with his truth.**
- **What is Righteousness and what is truth, according to scripture?**
- **Deut. 6:25** And it shall be our righteousness, **if we observe to do all these commandments** before Yahuah ^(Replaced with Lord/God)

our Elohim ^{(Mighty one(s)/God)}, as he has commanded us.

- **Isa. 51:7** Listen unto me, **you that know** righteousness, the people in whose heart *is* my law; fear you not the reproach of men, neither be you afraid of their revilings.
- **Psa. 119:142** Your righteousness *is* an everlasting righteousness, and your law *is* the truth.
- **Psa. 119:151** You *are* near, O Yahuah ^(Replaced with Lord/God); and all your commandments *are* truth.
  - o **Righteousness is keeping His Law's and Commandment's**
  - o **Truth is His Law's and Commandment's**

Joh. 12:48 He that rejects me, and receives not my words, has one that judge him: **the word that I have spoken, the same shall judge him in the last day**.

Rev. 19:11 And I saw heaven opened, and behold a white horse; and he that sat upon him *was* called **Faithful and True**, and in **righteousness** he does judge and make war.

CHAPTER 4

Col. 4:12 Epaphras greets you, he of you, a servants of Messiah, always striving for you in prayers, that you may stand full grown and being complete in every will of Elohim ^{(Mighty one(s)/God)}.

- Full grown is **5046.** τέλειος **teleios,** *tel'-i-os;* from **5056;** complete (in various applications of labor, growth, mental and moral character, etc.); neuter (as noun, with 3588) completeness: — of full age, man, perfect.
  - o Same word means perfect: Matt. 5:48 Be you therefore perfect, even as your Father which is in heaven is perfect.
    - ▪ Note worthy: The Greek word for full grown and perfect comes from a root word: **5056.** τέλος **telos,** *tel'-os;* from a primary τέλλω **tello** (to set out for a definite point or **goal**); properly, the **point aimed**....
    - ▪ This is where we get the English word telescope. Now let's read **Romans 10:4;** For Messi-

40

ah *is* the end of the law for righteousness to every one that believes. The word "End" in this verse is the Greek word τέλος **telos, which means focus or goal. So what Romans 10:4 is say is, Messiah is the Focus or goal of the Law, and not end as to do away with.**

- Complete is **4137.** πληρόω **pleroo,** *play-ro´-o;* from 4134; to make replete, i.e. (literally), level up (a hollow, verify (or coincide with a prediction), etc.: — accomplish, complete, fill (up), fulfil, preach, perfect, supply.
    - ○ Why is this important? Verse 12 said, "to be complete in Elohim ^{(Mighty one(s)/God)}", Right? This is the same Greek word in Matthew which says' "**Matt. 5:17** Think not that I am come to destroy the law, or the prophets: I am not come to destroy, but to **fulfill.**

        - ▪ Messiah came to preach it, fulfill what was spoken of Him. See *Luk. 24:43-45.* And verify, to make it complete. He made it replete by making it honorable. See *Isa. 42:21*

EPHESIANS

CHAPTER 2

We are saved by favor, not by doing the Law, we are saved to do the Law. Get it?

Eph. 2:8 For by favor you are saved, through faith, and this not of yourselves; *it is* the gift of Elohim ^{(Mighty one(s)/God)};
Eph. 2:9 not of works, that not anyone should boast;
Eph. 2:10 for we are *His* workmanship, created in Messiah Yahusha ^(replaced with Yeshua/Jesus) unto good works, which Elohim ^{(Mighty one(s)/God)} before prepared that we should walk in them.

- **Psa. 105:42** For He remembered His Holy Word *and* His servant Abraham;
- Psa. 105:43 and He brought His people out with joy; His elect with gladness.

41

- Psa. 105:44 And He gave to them the lands of the nations; and they inherited the labor of the peoples;
- **Psa. 105:45 so that they might observe His statutes and keep His laws. Praise Yahuah** ^(Replaced with Lord/God)!

- **Matt. 5:16** So let your light shine before men, so that they may see your good works, and may glory your Father in Heaven.

What is light?

Pro. 6:23 For the **commandment** *is* **a lamp; and the** law *is* **light**; and reproofs of instruction *are* the way of life:

Psa. 119:105 Your word *is* **a lamp unto my feet, and a light unto my path**.
- This was and is the Word that became flesh. This is how He walked Keeping the Commandments and the Law. This is also how we are suppose to walk. Did He not say, "take up your cross and follow"? *Matt. 16:24* We are also told that we should walk even as how He walked. *1Joh. 2:6*

Deut. 5:32 And you shall be careful to do as Yahuah ^(Replaced with Lord/God) your Elohim ^{(Mighty one(s)/God)} has commanded you; you shall not turn aside to the right or left.
Deut. 5:33 You shall walk in all the ways which Yahuah ^(Replaced with Lord/God) **your Elohim** ^{(Mighty one(s)/God)} **has commanded you, so that you may live**, and *that* good *may be* to you, and you may prolong *your* days in the land, which you will possess. *Deut. 4:40*

Psa. 119:1 Blessed *are* **the upright in the way, which walk in the Law of Yahuah** ^(Replaced with Lord/God).
Psa. 119:2 Blessed *are* those keeping His witnesses who seek Him with the whole heart.
Psa. 119:3 They also do not work evil; they walk in His way.

Paul is not teaching the Ephesians to be proud of being a Gentile

Eph. 2:11 Because of this, remember that you, the nations, *were* then in *the* flesh (those having been called Un-circumcision by those having been called Circumcision in the flesh made by hands)

Eph. 2:12 that at that time you were without Messiah, alienated from the commonwealth of Israel and strangers of the covenants of promise, having no hope and without Elohim (Mighty one(s)/God) in the world.

Eph. 2:13 But now, in Messiah Yahusha (replaced with Yeshua/Jesus) you who then were afar off, came to be near by the blood of Messiah.

Eph. 2:14 For He is our peace, He making us **both one**, and breaking down the middle wall of partition,

Eph. 2:15 in His flesh causing to cease the **enmity**, the Law of the commandments in **decree's** that He might in Himself create the two into one new man, making peace,

Eph. 2:16 and might reconcile both in one body to Elohim (Mighty one(s)/God) through the cross, slaying the enmity in Himself.

The key to understanding verse 15 is to look back at verse 14. The middle wall of partition, this was a wall separating Jews and Gentiles in the Temple.

Partition, G5418 φραγμος phragmos
Thayer Definition:
1) A hedge, a fence
2) That which separates, prevents two from coming together

This is not from the Law, but from the Oral law, Pharisaic traditions.

Acts 10:28 And he said to them, you know how unlawful it is for a man, a Jew, to unite with or to come near to one of another race. Yet Elohim (Mighty one(s)/God) showed to me not to call a man common or unclean.

- **Acts 10:28 - How that it is an unlawful thing** (hos athemiton estin). The conjunction hos is sometimes equivalent to hoti (that). The old form of athemitos was athemistos from themisto (themizo, themis , law custom) and a privative.

In the N.T. only here and 1Pet. 4:3 (Peter both times). **But there is no O.T. regulation forbidding such social contact with Gentiles,** though the rabbis had added it and had made it binding by custom. There is nothing more binding on the average person than social custom. On coming from the market an orthodox Jew was expected to

immerse to avoid defilement (Edersheim, *Jewish Social Life*, pp. 26-28;
Taylor's *Sayings of the Jewish Fathers*, pp. 15, 26, 137, second edition).

An unlawful thing (αθεμιτον)
The word is peculiar to Peter, being used only here and 1Pe 4:3. See note there. It emphasizes the violation of *established order,* being from the same root as τιθημι, to *lay down* or *establish.* The Jews professed to ground this prohibition on the Law of Moses; but there is no direct command in the Mosaic law forbidding Jews to associate with those of other nations. But Peter's statement is general, referring to the general practice of the Jews to separate themselves in common life from uncircumcised persons. Juvenal says that the Jews were taught by Moses "not to show the way except to one who practices the same rites, and to guide the circumcised alone to the well which they seek" (Sat., xiv., 104, 105). Tacitus also says of the Jews that "among themselves they are inflexibly faithful, and ready with charitable aid, but hate all others as enemies. They keep separate from all strangers in eating, sleeping, and matrimonial connections" ("Histories," v., 5).

Enmity

The original Greek manuscripts for **Ephesians 2:14-16**, as written in the Codices Sinaiticus, Alexandrinus, and Vaticanus, from *The Concordant Version of
the Sacred Scriptures,* Concordant Publishing Concern states:
* He for is the peace of us the one making the both one and the mid-wall of
  the barrier loosing the enmity in the flesh of Him the Law of the directions in
  decrees down-un-acting that the two He-should-be-creating in Self into one
  new human making peace and He-should-be-reconciling the both in the one
  body to the Father thru the pale from killing the enmity in it.

In the original Greek manuscripts it states, "Enmity in the flesh". In the flesh is missing from this verse in today's copy of the copied

Greek text in the "Bible". Let us take a closer look at this word from the Greek Lexicon to put this word in proper context.

189. ἔχθρα **echthra,** *ekh´-thrah;* **feminine of 2190**; hostility; by implication, a reason for opposition: — enmity, **hatred.**

- **2190.** ἐχθρός **echthros,** *ech-thros´;* from a primary ἔχθω **echtho** (to hate); hateful (passively, odious, or actively, hostile); usually as a noun, **an adversary (especially Satan): — enemy, foe.**

Looking at the Greek definition(s) this CANNOT be referring to the Law being understood as the Law or instruction(s) of The Most High.

We need to get a second witness from a different letter that Paul wrote:
- **Rom. 8:6** For to be carnally minded *is* death; but to be spiritually minded *is* life and peace.
  Rom. 8:7 Because the carnal mind *is* **enmity against Elohim** [(Mighty one(s)/God)]: **for it is not subject to the law of Elohim** [(Mighty one(s)/God)], neither indeed can be.
  Rom. 8:8 So then they that are in the **flesh cannot please Elohim** [(Mighty one(s)/God)].

So if we put Ephesians 2:15-16 (Original Greek text) with Romans 8:6-7, they are in perfect agreement.

What is a Saint?

Psa. 148:14 He also exalts the horn of his people, **the praise of all his saints; the children of Israel**, a people near unto him. Praise you Yahuah [(Replaced with Lord/God)].

Dan. 7:25 And he shall speak *great* words against the most High, and shall wear out the saints of the most High, and think to change times and laws: and they shall be given into his hand until a time and times and the dividing of time.

Rev. 14:12 Here is the **patience of the saints: here** *are* **they that keep the commandments of Elohim** [(Mighty one(s)/God)], **and the faith of Yahusha** [(replaced with Yeshua/Jesus)].

45

Eph. 2:21 in whom **all the building being fitted together** grows into a Holy temple in Yahuah ^(Replaced with Lord/God),

We are not separated into two bodies, Jews and Gentiles or Believers and Jews or
Hebrews and Gentiles etc….

GALATIANS

In the letter to the Galatians, many believe Paul is trying to warn them not to keep the Law. Is this so?

In **Galatians 6:13**, Paul specifically says that the "Judaizers" did not keep the Law. What "law" were they trying to burden the Galatians believers with?

Treasury of scripture knowledge notes on Galatians
Galatians -
The Galatians, or Gallo Grecians, were the descendants of Gaul's, who migrated from their own country, and after a series of disasters, got possession of a large district in Asia Minor, from them called Galatia (Pausanias, Attic. c. iv). They are mentioned by historians as a tall and valiant people, who went nearly naked, and used for arms only a buckler and sword; and the impetuosity of their attack is said to have been irresistible. Their religion, before their conversion was extremely corrupt and superstitious; they are said to have worshipped the mother of the gods, under the name of Adgistis; and to have offered human sacrifices of the prisoners they took in war. Believers appear to have been first planted in these regions by St. Paul himself (Gal 1:6; Gal 4:13); who visited the "churches" at least twice in that country (Acts 16:6; Acts 18:23). It is evident that this epistle was written soon after their reception of the good news, as he complains of their speedy apostasy from his doctrine (Gal 1:6); and as there is no notice of his second journey into that country, it has been supposed, with much probability, that it was written soon after his first, and consequently about AD 52 or 53. It appears that soon after the Apostle had left them, some Judaizing teachers intruded themselves into the churches; drawing them off from the true Good News, to depend on ceremonial

observances, and to the vain endeavor of "establishing their own righteousness."

Albert Barnes Introduction

The name "Galatia" is derived from the word Gaul, and was given to it because it had been conquered by the Gauls, who, having subdued the country, settled in it. - Pausanias, Attic. cap. iv. These were mixed with various Grecian families, and the country was also called Gallogroecia. - Justin, lib. xxiv. 4; xxv. 2; xvii. 3. This invasion of Asia Minor was made, according to Justin (lib. xxv. cap. 2), about the 479th year after the founding of Rome, and, of course, about 272 years before Messiah. They invaded Macedonia and Greece; and subsequently invaded Asia Minor, and became an object of terror to all that region. This expedition issued from Gaul, passed over the Rhine, along the Danube, through Noricum, Pannonia, and Moesia, and at its entrance into Germany, carried along with it many of the Tectosages. On their arrival in Thrace, Lutarius took them with him, crossed the Bosphorus, and effected the conquest of Asia Minor. - Liv. lib. xxxviii. c. 16. Such was their number, that Justin says, "they filled all Asia (i.e., all Asia Minor) like swarms of bees. Finally, they became so numerous that no kings of the east could engage in war without an army of Gauls; neither when driven from their kingdom could they flee to any other than to the Gauls. Such was the terror of the name of Gauls, and such the invincible felicity of their arms - *et armorum invicta felicitas erat* - that they supposed that in no other way could their own majesty be protected, or being lost, could be recovered, without the aid of Gallic courage. Their being called in by the king of Bithynia for aid, when they had gained the victory, they divided the kingdom with him, and called that region Gallogroecia." - Justin, xxv. 2. Under the reign of Augustus Cesar, about 26 years before the birth of Messiah, this region was reduced into the form of a Roman colony, and was governed by a proprietor, appointed by the emperor. They retained their original Gaulish language as late as the 5th century, as appears from the testimony of Jerome, who says that their dialect was nearly the same as that of the Treviri. - Tom. iv. p. 256. ed. Benedict. At the same time, they also spoke the Greek language in common with all the inhabitants of Lesser Asia, and therefore the Epistle to them was written in Greek, and was intelligible to them as well as to others. The Galatians, like the inhabitants of the surrounding country, were pagans, and their religion was of a gross and debasing kind. They are said to have worshipped "the mother of the gods," under the name of Agdistis. Callimachus, in his hymns, calls them "a foolish people." And Hillary, himself a Gaul, calls them Gallos indociles - expressions which, says Calmer, may well excuse Paul's addressing them as "foolish," Gal_3:1. There were few cities to be found among them, with the exception of Ancyra, Tavium, and Pessinus, which carried on some trade. It is not possible to ascertain the number of the inhabitants of Galatia, at the time when the good news was preached there, or when this Epistle was written. In 2 Macc. 8:20, it is said that Judas Maccabeus, exhorting his followers to fight manfully against the Syrians, referred to several instances of divine interposition to encourage them; and among others, "he told them of the battle which they had in Babylon with the Galatians; how they came but 8,000 in all to the business, with 4,000 Macedonians; and that the Macedonians being perplexed, the 8,000 destroyed 120,000, because of the help which they had from heaven, and so received a great booty." But it is not certain that this refers to those who dwelt in Galatia. It may refer to Gauls who at that time had overrun Asia Minor; the Greek word used here (Γαλατας Galatas), being taken equally for either. It is evident, however, that there was a large population that went under this general name; and it is probable that Galatia was thickly settled at the time when the good news was preached there. It was in the central part of Asia Minor, then one of the most densely-populated parts of the world, and was a region singularly fertile - Strabo, lib. xii. p. 567, 568, ed. Casaub. Many persons, also, were attracted there for the sake of commerce. That there were many Jews also, in all the provinces of Asia Minor, is apparent not only from the Acts of the Apostles, but is expressly declared by Josephus, Ant. xvi. 6.

The design of the whole Epistle, therefore, is to state and defend the true doctrine of justification, and to show that it did not depend on the observance of the laws of Moses. In the general purpose, therefore, it accords with the design of the Epistle to the Romans. In one respect, however, it differs from the design of that Epistle. That was written, to show that man could not be justified by any works of the Law, or by conformity to any law, moral or ceremonial; the object of this is, to show that justification cannot be obtained by conformity to the ritual or ceremonial law; or that

the observance of the ceremonial law is not necessary to salvation. In this respect, therefore, this Epistle is of less general interest than that to the Romans. It is also, in some respects, more difficult. The argument, if I may so express myself, is more Hebrew. It is more in the Hebraic manner; is designed to meet a Hebrew in his own way, and is, therefore, somewhat more difficult for all to follow. Still it contains great and vital statements on the doctrines of salvation, and, as such, demands the profound and careful attention of all who desire to be saved, and who would know the way of acceptance with Elohim ^{(Mighty one(s)/God)}.

According to Albert Barnes, the book of Galatians is written in Hebraic manner, this stands to reason considering Paul's background. It also stands to reason that in order to understand Galatians, one must have an understanding of Hebraic thought, without which much confusion will ensue.

CHAPTER 1

Gal. 1:2 and all the brothers with me, to the assemblies of Galatia.

Commentators argue whether Galatia were strictly Gentiles but the writings say that the dispersion was there.

1Pet. 1:1 Peter, an apostle of Yahusha ^(replaced with Yeshua/Jesus) Messiah, to *the* **elect sojourners of** *the* **dispersion** of Pontus, of **Galatia**, of Cappadocia, of Asia, and of Bithynia,

Jas. 1:1 James, a servant of Elohim ^{(Mighty one(s)/God)} and of Sovereign Yahusha ^(replaced with Yeshua/Jesus) Messiah, to the twelve tribes in the Dispersion, greeting:

Joh. 7:35 Then the Jews said amongst themselves, Where is this One about to go that we will not find Him? Is He about to go to the Dispersion of the Greeks, and to teach the Greeks?

Another Good News

Gal. 1:6 I wonder that you are so quickly turning back from the *One*

having called you by *the* favor of Messiah to another good news,
Gal. 1:7 which is not another; only there are some troubling you, even
determined to pervert the good news of Messiah.
Gal. 1:8 But even if we, or a angel out of Heaven, should preach good
news to you beside the good news we preached to you, let him be
accursed.

Paul also warns of another Yahusha ^(replaced with Yeshua/Jesus)

2Co. 11:3 But I fear lest by any means, as the serpent deceived Eve in
his craftiness, so your thoughts should be corrupted from the purity
which *is due* to Messiah.
2Co. 11:4 For if, indeed, the *one* coming proclaims another Yahusha
^(replaced with Yeshua/Jesus), whom we have not proclaimed, or *if* you receive
another spirit, which you have not received, or another good news,
which you never accepted, you might well endure *these*.

Paul refers to people troubling the Galatians, possibly a reference to
the Jerusalem council.

Acts 15:1 And going down from Judea, some taught the brothers,
saying, if you are not circumcised *according* to the custom of Moses,
you cannot be saved.

Acts 15:5 But some of those **rose up from the sect of the Pharisees**
who had believed, saying, It is necessary to circumcise them and to
command *them* to keep the Law of Moses.

Acts 15:24 Since we heard that some of us having gone out have
troubled you with words, unsettling your souls, saying, Be circumcised and keep the Law, to whom we gave no command;

Messiah warned us about the Pharisees

Matt. 16:11 How do you not perceive that *it was* not about loaves that
I said to you to take heed from the leaven of the Pharisees and Sadducees?
Matt. 16:12 Then they knew that He did not say to take heed from the
leaven of bread, but from the doctrine of the Pharisees and Sadducees.

Matt. 15:3 But answering He said to them, Why do you also transgress the command of Elohim ^{(Mighty one(s)/God)} on account of your tradition?

Messiah did not rebuke the Pharisees for keeping the Law, but for making their own law. The Pharisees believed in another law besides the written Word. They had what was called the "Oral Law". Which contained:
> **1) Halachot- New Laws derived from scripture**
> **2) Minhgim- Hebrew customs became law later by the majority.**
> **3) Takanot & Gezerot- Enactments & Decrees w/out scripture**
> **4) Maasim- works of righteousness, which becomes law.**

The writings say that the Pharisees did not keep Law:
> **Joh. 7:19**
> **Matt. 23:23**
> **Gal. 6:13**

Gal. 1:9 As we have said before, and now I say again, If anyone preaches a good news beside what you received, **let him be accursed.**
- **Deut. 27:26** Cursed *is* he who does not rise to all the Words of this Law, to do them! And all the people shall say, Amen!

Gal. 1:13 For you heard my way of life when *I was* in **Judaism**, that with surpassing *zeal* I persecuted the assembly of Elohim ^{(Mighty one(s)/God)} and ravaged it.

Gal. 1:14 And *I* progressed in Judaism beyond many contemporaries in my race, being much more a zealot of the **traditions** of my ancestors.

Acts 22:3 Indeed I am a man, a Jew having been born in Tarsus of Cilicia, but having been brought up in this city at the feet of Gamaliel, having been trained according to the exactness of the ancestral law, being a zealous one of Elohim ^{(Mighty one(s)/God)}, even as you all are today.

Notice the reference to the religion of the Jews is combined with

the traditions of the Fathers... the Oral Law.

Matt. 15:3 But answering He said to them, Why do you also transgress the command of Elohim ^{(Mighty one(s)/God)} on account of your tradition?

From John Gill's commentary
tradition: Tradition, in Latin *traditio* from *trado* I deliver, hand down, exactly agreeing with the original ¹αραδοσις [Strong's G3862], from ¹αραδιδωμι [Strong's G3860], I deliver, transmit.

Among the Jews it signifies what is called oral law, which they say has been successively handed down from Moses, through every generation, to Judah the Holy, who compiled and digested it into the Mishneh, to explain which of the two Gemaras, or Talmuds - called the Jerusalem and Babylonian - were composed. Of the estimation in which these were held by the Jews, the following may serve as an example: **"The words of the Scribes are lovely beyond the words of the law, for the words of the law are weighty and light, but the words of the Scribes are all weighty."**

CHAPTER 2

Gal. 2:3 But not even Titus, the *one* with me, a Greek, was compelled to be circumcised.

There is a lot of controversy over the issue of circumcision when it need not be. It seems as though there some who were saying you cannot be saved without circumcision.

Acts 15:1 And going down from Judea, some taught the brothers, *saying*, If you are not circumcised *according* to the custom of Moses, you cannot be saved.

Commentary from John Gill on Gal. 5:4
The Jews, who think they shall be saved for their circumcision, and that that will secure them from hell; they say no circumcised person goes down to hell, and that whoever is circumcised shall inherit the land; but there is none shall inherit the land, save a righteous person;

but everyone that is circumcised is called a righteous man; so that circumcision is their righteousness, on account of which they expect heaven and happiness. Shemot Rabba, sect. 19. fol. 104. 4. Zohar in Exod. fol. 10. 2.

Another thing to notice is the phrase custom of Moses, circumcision did not originate with Moses, it was with Abraham. As a sign of a covenant. See Genesis 17. What is taught here was referring to the oral law. If any Gentile were circumcised before hearing the truth, the Jews would not recognize their circumcision. It had to be by their custom.
     1) Hatafat Dan Brit – Drawing of Blood.
     2) Periah – Pulling Back of The Corona.
     3) Metsitsah – Sucking Blood.

Jos. 5:5 For all the people who had come out were circumcised. And **all the people who** *were* **born in the wilderness**, in the way, as they came out from Egypt, **had not been circumcised**.
Jos. 5:6 For the sons of Israel had walked forty years in the wilderness, until all the nation, the men of war who had come out of Egypt were consumed, *those* who did not listen to the voice of Yahuah [(Replaced with Lord/God)], to whom Yahuah [(Replaced with Lord/God)] had sworn to them not to show them the land which Yahuah [(Replaced with Lord/God)] swore to their fathers, to give to us, a land flowing with milk and honey; *these* were consumed.
Jos. 5:7 And He raised their sons up in their place. **Joshua circumcised them, for they had been uncircumcised; for they had not been circumcised in the way**.
Jos. 5:8 And it happened, when all the nation had finished being circumcised, they remained in their places in the camp until they revived.

Gal. 2:4 But *it was* because of those false brothers stealing in, who stole in to spy on our freedom which we have in Messiah Yahusha [(replaced with Yeshua/Jesus)], they desiring to enslave us,

Is Paul saying that our freedom in Yahusha [(replaced with Yeshua/Jesus)] **does not require us to do the Law (Circumcision)? Is the Law bondage or enslavement? Not according to the rest of the letters SIN enslaves, Not the Law.**

Joh. 8:32 And you will know the truth, and the truth will set you free.
Joh. 8:33 They answered Him, We are Abraham's seed, and we have been in slavery to no one, never! How do You say, You will become free?
Joh. 8:34 Yahusha ^(replaced with Yeshua/Jesus) answered them, truly, truly, I say to you, **Everyone practicing sin is a slave of sin.**
Joh. 8:35 But the slave does not remain in the house forever; the son remains to the age.
Joh. 8:36 Therefore, if the Son sets you free, you are free indeed.

Rom. 7:14 For we know that the Law is spiritual, but I am fleshly, having been **sold under sin.**

Gal. 4:4 But when the fullness of the time came, Elohim ^{(Mighty one(s)/God)} sent forth His Son, having come into being out of a woman, having come under Law,
Gal. 4:5 that He might redeem the ones under Law, **that we might receive the adoption of sons. (See Joh. 8:35-36)**

It is very sad that there are many who teach that the Law is Bondage and we are free from it. This leads them to continue in sin and become entangled in bondage all over again.

2Pe. 2:19 promising to them freedom, *though* themselves being slaves of corruption; for by whom anyone has been overcome, even to this one he has been enslaved.
2Pe. 2:20 For if by a recognition of Yahuah ^(Replaced with Lord/God) and Savior, Yahusha ^(replaced with Yeshua/Jesus) Messiah, *they* have escaped the defilements of the world, and again being entangled *they* have been overcome by these, *then their* last things have become worse *than* the first.
2Pe. 2:21 For it was better for them not to have recognized the way of righteousness than having recognized *it* to turn from the Holy commandment delivered to them.

We were in Bondage to the world and Sin, not the Law

Lev. 26:13 I *am* Yahuah ^(Replaced with Lord/God) your Elohim ^{(Mighty}

one(s)/God), who has brought you out from the land of the Egyptians, from being their slaves; and I will break the bars of your yoke, and cause you to stand erect.

Ex. 20:2 I *am* Yahuah ^(Replaced with Lord/God) your Elohim ^{(Mighty one(s)/God)}, who has brought you out from the land of Egypt, from the house of bondage.

If we apply common or mans reasoning to the following verses the scripture should say, Yahuah ^(Replaced with Lord/God) brought them (Us) out of bondage from Egypt so that He could put them (Us) into more Bondage, by giving us Sabbath(s) Laws and Commandments. Does this make any since? No Let us hear what the Word has to say.

Deut. 30:10 If you shall hearken unto the voice of Yahuah ^(Replaced with Lord/God) your Elohim ^{(Mighty one(s)/God)}, to keep his commandments and his statutes which are written in this book of the law, *and* if you turn unto Yahuah ^(Replaced with Lord/God) your Elohim ^{(Mighty one(s)/God)} with all your heart, and with all your soul.
Deut. 30:11 For this commandment which I command you this day, it *is* not hidden from you, neither *is* it far off.
Deut. 30:12 It *is* not in heaven, that you should say, Who shall go up for us to heaven, and bring it unto us, that we may hear it, and do it?
Deut. 30:13 Neither *is* it beyond the sea, that you should say, Who shall go over the sea for us, and bring it unto us, that we may hear it, and do it?
Deut. 30:14 But the word *is* very nigh unto you, in your mouth, and in your heart, that you may do it.

The Most High was not asking for much at all. He wanted Israel to keep His commandments and laws in their Heart and in their mouth. He wants us to speak, teach obey etc. His Word. But it must start from your Heart.

1John 5:2 By this we know that we love the children of Elohim ^{(Mighty one(s)/God)}, when we love Elohim ^{(Mighty one(s)/God)}, and keep his commandments.
1John 5:3 For this is the love of Elohim ^{(Mighty one(s)/God)}, that we keep

55

his commandments: and his commandments are not grievous.

Deut. 5:15 And remember that you were a slave in the land of Egypt, and Yahuah ^(Replaced with Lord/God) your Elohim ^{(Mighty one(s)/God)} brought you out from there by a mighty hand and by a stretched out arm. On account of this Yahuah ^(Replaced with Lord/God) your Elohim ^{(Mighty one(s)/God)} has commanded you to keep the Sabbath day.

Deut. 15:15 And you shall remember that you were a slave in the land of Egypt, and Yahuah ^(Replaced with Lord/God) your Elohim ^{(Mighty one(s)/God)} redeemed you. On account of this I command you this thing today.

Gal. 2:12 For before some came from James, he ate with the nations. But when they came, he drew back and separated himself, being afraid of those of the circumcision.

Acts 10:28 And he said to them, You know how unlawful it is for a man, a Jew, to unite with or to come near to one of another race. Yet Elohim ^{(Mighty one(s)/God)} showed to me not to call a man common or unclean.

John Gill's commentary on Acts 10:28
it was prohibited to eat and drink any sort of liquor with them in their houses, nor might they walk with them in the streets, or on the road; says Maimonides,
"it is forbidden a Jew to unite himself to Gentiles, because they are suspected of shedding blood, and he may not join himself with them in the way; if he meets a Gentile in the way, he causes him to turn to the right hand; if they ascend by an ascent, or descend by a descent, the Israelite may not be below, and the Gentile above: but the Israelite must be above, and the Gentile below, lest he should fall upon him and kill him; and he may not go even with (or along side by him) lest he break his skull."
It is said of some Rabbis, that they saw a certain man coming; "says R. Chiyah, let us be gone, perhaps this man is an idolatrous Gentile, or one of the people of the earth, and it is forbidden to join with him in the way." They looked upon the houses of Gentiles unclean, and therefore would not enter into them: See Gill on Joh. 18:28. yea they say, that: "the court of a stranger (or Gentile) is as the habitation of a

56

beast." Such an aversion was there in that people to all civil society with Gentiles: and so Apoltonius says of them, that "they not only departed from the Romans, but from all men, living a separate life from others; nor did they communicate at table with others; neither in things sacred, nor in any ceremonies;" and this was well known to Jews and Gentiles:

- **This is not according to scriptures**

Isa. 9:1 Yet there *shall not* be gloom for which anguish *is* to her *as in* the former time *when* He degraded the land of Zebulon, and the land of Naphtali so afterwards He will glory the way of the sea, beyond the Jordan, **Galilee of the nations.**
Isa. 9:2 The people who walk in darkness have seen a great light. The ones who dwell in the land of the shadow of death, light has shone on them.

Gal. 2:13 And also the rest of the Jews dissembled with him, so as even Barnabas was led away with their dissembling. **BARNABAS WAS A LEVITE**
- **Acts 4:36** And Joses, the *one* surnamed Barnabas by the apostles, which being translated is, Son of Consolation, a Levite, a Cypriot by race,
Gal. 2:14 But when I saw that they did not walk uprightly with the truth of the good news, I said to Peter before all, If you being a Jew [G2453], live heathen-like, and not *as the* Jews [G2452], why do you compel *the* nations to Judaize [G2450]?

This is the only time this word is used, All other times Jews is translated
Ioudaios G2453
G2452 Ιουδςαι. κω Ioudaikos
Thayer Definition:
1) after the manner of the Jews

The sense of this word seems to be a Judaizer...not a Jew. A Judaizer is a follower of oral law, a Jew is not necessarily so. To live as do the Jews (Ιουδαι.|ζειν)
N.T. Once in lxx, Est_8:17. Also in Joseph. *B. J.* 2:18, 2, and Plut. *Cic.*

7. It is used by Ignatius, *Magn.* x.

Χριστιανιζειν *to practice Christianity* occurs in Origen.

This is the only time the term Judaize is used in all of the writings.
This is interesting that it was referring to Peter and Barnabas following
the Oral law and not Law in this letter.

G2450 Ιουδαι.ζω Ioudaizo
Thayer Definition:
1) to adopt Jewish customs and rites, imitate the Jews, Judaise

Gal. 2:15 We, **Jews** [(G2553)] by nature & not sinners of the nations,
Gal. 2:16 knowing that a man is not justified by works of Law, but
that *it is* through faith *in* Yahusha [(replaced with Yeshua/Jesus)] Messiah we also
believed into Messiah Yahusha [(replaced with Yeshua/Jesus)], that we may be
justified by faith *in* Messiah and not by works of Law,
(because no flesh can be justified by works of Law). *Psa. 123:2*

**Paul is saying that the Jews know that the Law cannot justify
them…**

Psa. 123:2 Behold, as the eyes of servants *look* to the hand of their
sovereigns; as the eyes of a maiden to the hand of her mistress; so our
eyes *wait* on Yahuah [(Replaced with Lord/God)] our Elohim [(Mighty one(s)/God)],
until He shows favor to us.

Psa. 143:1 *A Psalm of David.* Hear my prayer, O Yahuah [(Replaced with
Lord/God)] give ear to my supplications; answer me in Your faithfulness,
in Your righteousness;
Psa. 143:2 and do not enter into judgment with Your servant, for not
anyone living is just in Your sight.

Rom. 9:31 but Israel following after a Law of righteousness did not
arrive at a Law of righteousness?
Rom. 9:32 Why? Because *it was* not of faith, but as of works of Law.
For they stumbled at the Stone-of-stumbling,
Rom. 9:33 as it has been written, "Behold, I place in" "Zion a Stone-
of-stumbling," "and a Rock-of-offense," "and everyone believing on
Him will not be shamed." *LXX and MT -Isa. 28:16; MT -Isa. 8:14*
Rom. 10:1 Brothers, truly my heart's pleasure and supplication to

Elohim ^{(Mighty one(s)/God)} on behalf of Israel is for *it* to be saved.
Rom. 10:2 For I witness to them that they have zeal to Elohim ^{(Mighty one(s)/God)}, but not according to knowledge.
Rom. 10:3 For being ignorant of the righteousness of Elohim ^{(Mighty one(s)/God)}, and seeking to establish their own righteousness, they did not submit to the righteousness of Elohim ^{(Mighty one(s)/God)}.
Rom. 10:4 For Messiah *is* the **end** of Law for righteousness to everyone that believes.

- **5056.** τέλος **telos**, *tel´-os;* from a primary τέλλω **tello** (to set out for a definite **point or goal**); **properly, the point aimed at as a limit**, i.e.

Rom. 10:5 For Moses writes *of* the righteousness *which is* of the Law: "The man doing these things shall live by them." *Lev. 18:5*
Rom. 10:6 But the righteousness of faith says this: "Do not say in your heart, Who will go up into Heaven?" (that is to bring down Messiah);
Rom. 10:7 or, "Who will go down into the abyss?" (that is, to bring Messiah up from *the* dead.)
Rom. 10:8 But what does it say? "The Word is near you, in your mouth and in your heart" (that is, the Word of faith which we proclaim) *Deut. 30:12-14*.

Php. 3:5 in circumcision, *the* eighth day, of *the* race of Israel *the* tribe of Benjamin, a Hebrew of the Hebrews; according to Law, a Pharisee;
Php. 3:6 according to zeal, persecuting the assembly; according to righteousness in Law, being blameless.
Php. 3:7 But what things were gain to me, these I have counted loss because of Messiah.
Php. 3:8 But, no, rather I also count all things to be loss because of the Excellency of the knowledge of Messiah Yahusha ^(replaced with Yeshua/Jesus) my Sovereign, for whose sake I have suffered the loss of all things and count *them to be* trash, that I might gain Messiah
Php. 3:9 and be found in Him; **not having my own righteousness of Law, but through the faith of Messiah,** *having* **the righteousness of Elohim** ^{(Mighty one(s)/God)} **on faith,**

On Judgment Day we can stand there with our garments of Righteousness on.

Isa. 64:6 But we are all as the unclean *thing*, and all our righteousness's *are* as a menstruation cloth. And we all fade as a leaf, and like the wind our iniquities take us away.

Matt. 22:10 And going out into the highways, those slaves gathered all as many as they found, both evil and good. And the wedding feast was filled with reclining guests.
Matt. 22:11 And the king coming in to look over those reclining, he saw a man there not having been dressed *in* a wedding garment.
Matt. 22:12 And he said to him, Friend, how did you come in here, not having a wedding garment? But he was speechless.

The Garments of Salvation

Isa. 61:10 Rejoicing I will rejoice in Yahuah [(Replaced with Lord/God)]. My soul shall be joyful in my Elohim [(Mighty one(s)/God)]. For He clothed me *with* garments of salvation; He put on me the robe of righteousness, even as a bridegroom decks as a priest *his* ornament, and as a bride wears her ornaments.

Gal. 2:17 But if seeking to be justified in Messiah, we ourselves also were found *to be* sinners, *is* Messiah then a minister of sin? Let it not be!
Gal. 2:18 For what if I build again these things, which I destroyed, I confirm myself *as* a transgressor.
Gal. 2:19 For through Law I died to Law, that I might live to Elohim [(Mighty one(s)/God)].

Gal. 2:20 I have been crucified with Messiah, and I live; *yet* no longer, I but Messiah lives in me. And the *life* I now live in the flesh, I live by faith toward the Son of Elohim [(Mighty one(s)/God)], the *One* loving me and giving Himself over on my behalf.
Gal. 2:21 I do not set aside the favor of Elohim [(Mighty one(s)/God)]; for **if** righteousness *is* through Law, then Messiah died without cause.

This seems to be a difficult saying of Paul for some. Let's cross-reference this with some other writings.

Col. 3:1 If, then, you were raised with Messiah, seeks the things above, where Messiah is sitting at *the* right of Elohim [(Mighty one(s)/God)];

Psa.110:1

Col. 3:2 set your affection on things above, not the things on the earth.
Col. 3:3 For you died, and your life has been hidden with Messiah in Elohim ^{(Mighty one(s)/God)}.
Col. 3:4 Whenever Messiah our life is revealed, then also you will be revealed with Him in glory.
Col. 3:5 Then put to death your members, which *are* on the earth: fornication, uncleanness, passion, evil lust, and covetousness, which is idolatry;
Col. 3:6 on account of which things the wrath of Elohim ^{(Mighty one(s)/God)} is coming on the sons of disobedience,

1Pe. 2:24 who "Himself carried up in His body our sins" onto the tree; that dying to sins, we might live to righteousness, of whom "*by* His wound you were healed."

Rom. 8:10 But if Messiah *is* in you, **the body indeed *is* dead because of sin**, but the Spirit *is* life because of righteousness.
Rom. 8:11 But if the Spirit of the *One* having raised Yahusha ^(replaced with Yeshua/Jesus) from *the* dead dwells in you, the *One* having raised the Messiah from *the* dead will also make your mortal bodies live through the indwelling of His Spirit in you.
Rom. 8:12 So, then, brothers, we are debtors, not to the flesh, to live according to flesh,
Rom. 8:13 for if you live according to flesh, you are going to die. But if by *the* Spirit you put to death the practices of the body, you will live.
Rom. 8:14 For as many as are led by *the* Spirit of Elohim ^{(Mighty one(s)/God)}, these are sons of Elohim ^{(Mighty one(s)/God)}.
Rom. 6:11 So also you count yourselves to be truly dead to sin, but alive to Elohim ^{(Mighty one(s)/God)} in Messiah Yahusha ^(replaced with Yeshua/Jesus) our Sovereign.
Rom. 6:12 Then do not let sin reign in your mortal body, to obey it in its lusts.
Rom. 6:13 Neither present your members *as* instruments of unrighteousness to sin, but present yourselves to Elohim ^{(Mighty one(s)/God)} as *one* living from *the* dead, and your member's instruments of righteousness to Elohim ^{(Mighty one(s)/God)}.
Rom. 6:14 For your sin shall not sovereign it over you, for you are not under Law, but under favor.

61

Rom. 6:15 What then? Shall we sin because we are not under Law, but under favor? Let it not be!

Rom. 6:16 Do you not know that to whom you present yourselves *as* slaves for obedience, you are slaves to whom you obey, whether of sin to death, or obedience to righteousness?

Rom. 6:17 But thanks *be* to Elohim ^{(Mighty one(s)/God)} that you were slaves of sin, but you obeyed from *the* heart the form of doctrine to which you were delivered.

Rom. 6:18 And having been set free from sin, you were enslaved to righteousness.

Rom. 6:19 I speak as a man on account of the weakness of your flesh. For as you presented your members *as* **slaves to uncleanness and to lawless Acts unto lawless Acts, so now yield your members as slaves to righteousness unto sanctification.**

Rom. 6:20 For **when you were slaves of sin, you were free as to righteousness**.

Rom. 6:21 Therefore what fruit did you have then *in the things* over which you are now ashamed? For the end of those things *is* death.

Rom. 6:22 But now having been set free from sin, and having been enslaved to Elohim ^{(Mighty one(s)/God)}, you have your fruit unto sanctification, and the end everlasting life.

Rom. 6:23 For the wages of sin *is* death, but the gift of Elohim ^{(Mighty one(s)/God)} *is* everlasting life in Messiah Yahusha ^(replaced with Yeshua/Jesus) our Sovereign.

Does Following the Law Lead to Death?

Deut. 30:16 in that I *am* commanding you today to love Yahuah ^(Replaced with Lord/God) your Elohim ^{(Mighty one(s)/God)}, to walk in His ways, and to keep His commands and His statutes, and His judgments, and **you shall live and multiply**, and Yahuah ^(Replaced with Lord/God) your Elohim ^{(Mighty one(s)/God)} shall bless you in the land where you are going in, to possess it.

Sin Kills Not the Law

Ezek. 18:4 Behold, they *are* all My souls. As the soul of the father, also the soul of the son, they *are* Mine. The soul that sins, it shall die.

Rom. 7:1 Or are you ignorant brothers, (for I speak to those knowing Law,) that the Law sovereign it over the man for as long a time as he lives?

Rom. 7:2 For the married woman was bound by Law to the living husband; but if the husband dies, she is set free from the Law of the husband.

Rom. 7:3 So then, *if* the husband *is* living, she will be called an adulteress if she becomes another man's. But if the husband dies, she is free from the Law, *so as for* her not to be an adulteress *by* becoming another man's.

Rom. 7:4 So that, my brothers, you also were made dead to the Law through the body of Messiah, for you to become Another's, to *the One* raised from *the* dead, so that we may bear fruit to Elohim ^{(Mighty one(s)/God)}.

Rom. 7:5 For when we were in the flesh, the passions of sin were working in our members through the Law for the bearing of fruit unto death.

Rom. 7:6 But now we have been set free from the Law, having died *to that* in which we were held, so as *for* us to serve in newness of spirit, and not *in* oldness of letter.

Rom. 7:7 What shall we say then? *Is* the Law sin? Let it not be! But I did not know sin except through Law; for also I did not know lust except the Law said, "You shall not lust." *Ex. 20:17*

Rom. 7:8 But sin taking occasion through the commandment worked every lust in me; for apart from Law, sin *is* dead.

Rom. 7:9 And I was alive apart from Law once, but the commandment came, and sin came alive, and I died.

Rom. 7:10 And the commandment which *was* to life, this was found *to be* death to me;

Rom. 7:11 for sin taking occasion through the commandment deceived me, and through it killed *me*.

Rom. 7:12 So indeed the Law *is* Holy and the commandment Holy and just and good.

Rom. 7:13 Then that *which is* good, *has it* become death to me? Let it not be! But sin, that it might appear *to be* sin, having worked out death to me through the good, in order that sin might become excessively sinful through the commandment

Rom. 7:14 For we know that the Law is spiritual but I am fleshly, having been sold under sin.

Rom. 7:15 For what I work out I do not know. For what I do not will this I do. But what I hate, this I do.

Rom. 7:16 But if I do what I do not will I agree with the Law, that *it is* good.

Rom. 7:17 But now I no longer work it out, but the sin dwelling in me.

Rom. 7:18 For I know that in me, that is in my flesh, dwells no good. For to will is present to me, but to work out the good I do not find.

Rom. 7:19 For what good I desire, I do not do. But the evil I do not desire, this I do.

Rom. 7:20 But if I do what I do not desire, *it is* no longer I working it out, but the sin dwelling in me.

Rom. 7:21 I find then the law, *when* I desire to do the right, that evil is present with me.

Rom. 7:22 For I delight in the Law of Elohim ^{(Mighty one(s)/God)} according to the inward man;

Rom. 7:23 but I see another law in my members having warred against the law of my mind, and taking me captive by the law of sin being in my members.

Rom. 7:24 O wretched man *that* I *am*! Who shall deliver me from the body of this death?

Rom. 7:25 I thank Elohim ^{(Mighty one(s)/God)} through Yahusha ^(replaced with Yeshua/Jesus) Messiah our Sovereign! So then I myself with the mind truly serve *the* Law of Elohim ^{(Mighty one(s)/God)}, *with* the flesh *the* law of sin.

Could Paul be saying through the Written Law, I Died to the Oral law?

Col. 2:20 If, then, you died with Messiah from **the elements of the world,** why are you under *its* decrees, as living in *the* world?

Col. 2:21 Do not handle, do not taste, do not touch,

Col. 2:22 which things are all for corruption in the using, according to the "**injunctions and teachings of men.**" *Isa. 29:13*

CHAPTER 3

Gal. 3:2 This only I desire to learn from you: Did you receive the Spirit by works of Law or by hearing of faith?

Gal. 3:3 Are you so foolish? Having begun in *the* Spirit, do you now perfect *yourself* in the flesh?

Following the Law is not walking in the Flesh.

Rom. 7:14 For we know that the Law is spiritual but I am fleshly, having been sold under sin.

Earning Salvation through works of the Flesh.

Gen. 3:7 And the eyes of both of them were opened, and they knew that they *were* naked. And they sewed leaves of the fig tree, and made girdles for themselves.

Being justified by works

Rom. 3:28 Then we conclude a man to be justified by faith without works of Law.
Rom. 3:29 Or *is He* the Elohim ^{(Mighty one(s)/God)} of Jews only, and not also of the nations? Yes, of the nations also,
Rom. 3:30 since *it is* one Elohim ^{(Mighty one(s)/God)} who will justify circumcision by faith, and un-circumcision through faith.
Rom. 3:31 Then *is* the Law annulled through faith? Let it not be! But we establish Law.

This does not mean we do not do works, since we are walking by Faith. Our Faith will produce works through Law by FAITH

Jas. 2:17 So also faith, if it does not have works, is dead being by itself.
Jas. 2:18 But someone will say, You have faith, and I have works. Show me your faith apart from your works, and I will show you my faith out of my works.
Jas. 2:19 You believe that Elohim ^{(Mighty one(s)/God)} is One .You do well even the demons believe and shudder
Jas. 2:20 But are you willing to know, O vain man, that faith apart from works is dead?
Jas. 2:21 Was not our father Abraham justified by works offering up his son Isaac on the altar? *Gen. 22:9*
Jas. 2:22 You see that faith worked with his works and out of the works the faith was made perfected.

Jas. 2:23 And the **Scripture** was fulfilled, saying, "And Abraham believed Elohim ^{(Mighty one(s)/God)}, and it was counted for righteousness to him;" and he was called, Friend of Elohim ^{(Mighty one(s)/God)}. *Gen. 15:6; Isa. 41:8*

Jas. 2:24 You see, then, that a man is justified out of works, and not out of faith only.

Jas. 2:25 But in the same way Rahab the harlot was also justified out of works, having received the messengers, and sending them out by another way.

Jas. 2:26 For as the body is dead apart from the spirit, so also faith is dead apart from works.

We are given the Spirit by Faith and not by works

Psa. 51:10 Create in me a clean heart, O Elohim ^{(Mighty one(s)/God)}; and renew a steadfast spirit within me.

Psa. 51:11 Do not cast me out from Your presence, and do not take Your Holy Spirit from me.

Psa. 51:12 Restore to me the joy of Your salvation, and uphold me *with* a willing spirit

Psa. 51:13 *Then* I will teach transgressors Your ways; and sinners will turn back to You.

Psa. 51:14 Deliver me from the guilt of shedding blood, O Elohim ^{(Mighty one(s)/God)}, O Elohim ^{(Mighty one(s)/God)} of my salvation; my tongue shall sing aloud of Your righteousness.

Gal. 3:5 Then He supplying the Spirit to you and working works of power in you, *is it* by works of Law or by hearing of faith?

- **Zech. 4:6** Then he answered and spoke to me, saying, This *is* the Word of Yahuah ^(Replaced with Lord/God) to Zerubbabel saying, Not by might nor by power, but by My Spirit says Yahuah ^(Replaced with Lord/God) of Hosts.

Gal. 3:6 Even "as Abraham believed Elohim ^{(Mighty one(s)/God)}, and it was counted to him for righteousness," *Gen 15:6*

Gal. 3:7 know, then, that those of faith, these are sons of Abraham.

Gal. 3:8 And the Scripture foreseeing that Elohim ^{(Mighty one(s)/God)} would justify the nations by faith, **preached the good news before to Abraham**: "All the nations will be blessed" "in you." *Gen. 12:3*

Gal. 3:9 So that those of faith are blessed with the faithful Abraham.
Gal. 3:10 For as many as are out of works of Law, *these* are under a curse. For it has been written, "Cursed *is* everyone who does not continue in all the things having been written in the book of the Law, to do them." *Deut. 27:26*
Gal. 3:11 And that no one is justified by Law before Elohim ^{(Mighty one(s)/God)} *is* clear because, "The just shall live by faith." *Hab. 2:4*

- Faith, and having the Spirit is not a new concept on the Old Testament. I originated their and carried through to the messianic writings

Is Following the Law A CURSE?

Isa. 24:5 And the earth is profaned under those living in it, because they transgress laws and violate a statute, and break the everlasting covenant.

Isa. 24:6 On account of this a curse has devoured the land; and they who live in it are held guilty. For this those living in the land are consumed, and few men are left.
Neh. 9:28 But after a rest to them, they turned to doing evil before You. And You left them in the hand of their enemies, and they ruled over them. But they came back and cried to You, and You heard them from Heaven, and You saved them according to Your mercies.
Neh. 9:29 And You witnessed against them to bring them again to Your Law, but they acted presumptuously, and did not listen to Your command's but *were* against Your judgments they sinned in them, which if a man does he shall live in them. And they gave a rebellious shoulder, and hardened their neck, and would not hear.

John 7:49 But this people who knows not the law are cursed.

The curse comes from those Transgressing the Law and Commandments

Deut. 27:26 Cursed *is* he who does not rise to all the Words of this Law, to do them! And all the people shall say, Amen!

Deut. 28:15 But it shall come to pass, if you will not hearken unto the voice of Yahuah ^(Replaced with Lord/God) your Elohim ^{(Mighty one(s)/God)}, to observe to do all his commandments and his statutes which I command you this day; that all these curses shall come upon you, and overtake you:

Psa. 119:21 You have rebuked the proud *that are* cursed, which do err from your commandments.

Psa. 119:30 I have chosen the way of truth ^(EMUNAH); I have held Your judgments level

Psa. 119:86 All Your Commands *are* faithful they persecute me *with* lying; help me!

Psa. 119:138 You have enjoined Your witnesses *as* righteous and very faithful

Matt. 23:23 Woe to you, scribes and Pharisees, hypocrites! For you pay tithes of mint and Dill and Cummin, and you have left aside the weightier *matters* of the Law: judgment, and mercy, and faith. It was right to do these, and not to have left those aside.

Rom. 3:31 Then *is* the Law annulled through faith? Let it not be! But we establish Law.

Young's Literal Translation

Gal. 3:12 and the law is not by faith, but…The man who did them shall live in them.
Gal. 3:13 Messiah redeemed us from **the curse of the Law**, having become a curse for us; for it has been written, "Cursed *is* everyone having been hung on a tree;" *Deut. 21:23*
Gal. 3:14 that the blessing of Abraham might be to the nations in Messiah Yahusha ^(replaced with Yeshua/Jesus), that we might receive the promise of the Spirit through faith.
Gal. 3:15 Brothers, I speak according to man, a covenant having been ratified, even *among* mankind, no one sets aside or adds to *it*.
Gal. 3:16 But the promises were spoken to Abraham and to his Seed (it does not say, And to seeds, as of many, but as of one, "And to your

Seed," which is Messiah). *Genesis 3:15; 21:12; 22:18, Rom. 9:6; Heb. 11:18*

Gal. 3:17 And I say this, a covenant having been ratified before to Messiah by Elohim ^{(Mighty one(s)/God)}, *the* Law coming into being **four hundred and thirty years after** does not annul the promise, so as to abolish *it.*

Gal. 3:18 For if the inheritance *is* of Law, *it is* no more of promise; but Elohim ^{(Mighty one(s)/God)} has given *it* to Abraham through promise.

Gal. 3:19 Why the Law then? It was for the sake of transgressions, until the Seed should come, to whom it had been promised, being ordained through angels in a mediator's hand.

Was the Law 430 Years After What? The Law spoken of Here by Paul was added Because of Transgressions. Transgressions of What? Let's take a look

1 John 3:4 Whosoever commits sin transgresses also the law: for sin is the transgression of the law.

- According to this verse, Sin means transgression of the Law. Let's look up the word Transgression.
- **458.** ἀνομία **anomia,** *an-om-ee´-ah;* from <u>459</u>; illegality, i.e. violation of law or (genitive case) wickedness: — iniquity, x transgress(-ion of) the law, unrighteousness.

   - <u>459</u>. ἄνομος **anomos,** *an´-om-os;* from 1 (as a negative particle) and 3551; lawless, i.e. (negatively) not subject to (the Jewish) law; (by implication, a Gentile), or (positively) wicked: — **without law, lawless, transgressor, unlawful, wicked.**
   - Transgression by definition means, one that is Lawless, Who's Law? The Creators Laws. Transgressing the Creators Laws is considered WICKED and UNRIGHTEOUS. The one that does not keep The Fathers Laws is SINNING and is UNRIGHTEOUS, and WICKED. Is this what you want to be in the eye's of the Father?
   - So 1Joh. 3:4 can be read as the following: Everyone practicing sin also practices lawlessness, and sin is lawlessness.

Rom. 4:13 For the promise *was* not through Law to Abraham, or to his seed, *for* him to be the heir of the world, but through a righteousness of faith.

Rom. 4:14 For if those of Law *are* heirs, faith has been made of no effect, and the promise has been annulled.

Rom. 4:15 For the Law works out wrath; **for where no law is, neither *is* transgression.**

Rom. 4:16 On account of this, *it is* of faith, that *it be* according to favor, for the promise to be certain to all the seed, not to that of the Law only, but also to that of *the* faith of Abraham, who is father of us all

Rom. 5:13 For sin was in *the* world until Law, but sin is not charged *where* there is no law;

Rom. 5:14 but death reigned from Adam until Moses, even on those who had not sinned in the likeness of Adam's transgression, who is a type of the coming *One.*

Rom. 5:15 But the free gift *is* not also like the trespasses. For if by the trespasses of the one the many died, much more the favor of Elohim ^{(Mighty one(s)/God)}, and the gift in favor, which *is* of the one Man, Yahusha ^(replaced with Yeshua/Jesus) Messiah, did abound to the many.

Rom. 5:16 And the gift *is* not as by one having sinned; for indeed the judgment *was* of one to condemnation, but the free gift *is* of many trespasses to justification.

Rom. 5:17 For if by the deviation of the one death reigned through the one, much more those who are receiving the abundance of favor and the gift of righteousness shall rule in life by the One, Yahusha ^(replaced with Yeshua/Jesus) Messiah.

Rom. 5:18 So then, as through one deviation *it was* toward all men to condemnation, so also through one righteous Acts toward all men to justification of life.

Rom. 5:19 For as through the one man's disobedience the many were constituted sinners, so also through the obedience of the One the many shall be constituted righteous.

Rom. 5:20 But Law came in besides that the trespasses might abound. But where sin abounded, favor much more abounded,

Rom. 6:23 For the wages of sin *is* death, but the gift of Elohim ^{(Mighty} ^{one(s)/God)} *is* everlasting life in Messiah Yahusha ^(replaced with Yeshua/Jesus) our Sovereign.

Abraham Kept the Commandments and Laws, So the question is, How did He do that (Keep the Commandments and Laws) if it wasn't added till 430 Years Later?

- **Gen. 26:5** because Abraham listened to My voice and heeded My charge, My commands, My statutes, and My laws.

The Law Spoken of Here is the Law of Sacrifices

Jer. 7:22 For I did not speak to your fathers, nor command them in the day that I brought them out from the land of Egypt concerning matters of burnt offerings and sacrifices
Jer. 7:23 But I commanded them this thing, saying, Obey My voice, and I will be your Elohim ^{(Mighty one(s)/God)}, and you shall be My people. Also, Walk in all the ways that I have commanded you, so that it may be well with you.

Psa. 51:16 For you desire not sacrifice; else would I give *it*: you delight not in burnt offering.

Psa. 40:6 Sacrifices and offering you did not desire; mine ears have you opened: burnt offering and sin offering have you not required.
Psa. 40:7 Then said I, Lo, I come: in the volume of the book *it is* written of me,

The Father desired obedience Not Sacrifices or SIN offerings or burnt offerings. But Because of SIN these were instituted or ADDED. Added where? The LAW. Psa. Tells of there was a need for one to come in the volume of the Book, which was written of Him. Who is "Me" in verse 7? Let's take a look:

- **Luke 24:44** And he said unto them, These *are* the words which I spoke unto you, while I was yet with you, that all things must be fulfilled, which were **written in the law of Moses, and in the prophets, and in the psalms, concerning me**.
- **Luke 24:45** Then opened he their understanding, that they might understand the scriptures,

Yahusha ^(replaced with Yeshua/Jesus) came to put a stop to the Sacrificial system concerning SIN Offering's and burnt offerings, also to teach us as well, to be obedient, which was what He wanted all along. So the Sin Offering and Burnt Offering were **Added** and offered according to the Law.

- **Heb. 10:6** In burnt offerings and *sacrifices* for sin you have had no pleasure.
  Heb. 10:7 Then said I, Lo, I come (in the volume of the book it is written of me,) to do your will, O Elohim ^{(Mighty one(s)/God)}.
  Heb. 10:8 Above when he said, Sacrifice and offering and burnt offerings and *offering* for sin you would not, neither had pleasure *therein*; which are offered by the law;

When did this change take place? In Exodus Chapter 32. Israel Worshipped the golden calf made at the bottom of Mount Sinai. Let's see what happened after the golden calf:

- **Ex. 32:26** Then Moses stood in the gate of the camp, and said, Who *is* on Yahuah's ^(Replaced with Lord/God) side? *let him come* unto me. And **all the sons of Levi gathered themselves together unto him.**
  Ex. 32:27 And he said unto them, Thus says Yahuah ^(Replaced with Lord/God) Elohim ^{(Mighty one(s)/God)} of Israel, Put every man his sword by his side, *and* go in and out from gate to gate throughout the camp, and slay every man his brother, and every man his companion, and every man his neighbor.
  Ex. 32:28 And the children of Levi did according to the word of Moses: and there fell of the people that day about three thousand men.

Because of what the Levites did, a change was made. Initially The Firstborn was to be Holy to the Most High. But it was changed because of Sin that was done at Mount Sinai.

- **Num. 3:12** And I, behold, I have taken the Levites from among the children of Israel instead of all the firstborn that open the matrix among the children of Israel: therefore the Levites shall be mine;

I pray this shed some light on the subject. Paul was not talking about the Law itself, but what was added to the Law "Sin Offerings & Burnt Offerings".

Gal. 3:21 Then is the Law against the promises of Elohim ^{(Mighty one(s)/God)}? Let it not be! For if a law had been given which had been able to make alive, indeed righteousness would have been out of Law.
Gal. 3:22 But the Scripture locked up all under sin, that the promise by faith of Yahusha ^(replaced with Yeshua/Jesus) Messiah might be given to the ones believing.
Gal. 3:23 But before the coming of faith, we were guarded under Law, having been locked up to the faith being about to be revealed.
Gal. 3:24 So that the Law has become a trainer of us *until* Messiah, that we might be justified by faith.
Gal. 3:25 But faith coming, we are no longer under a trainer;
Gal. 3:26 for you are all sons of Elohim ^{(Mighty one(s)/God)} through faith in Messiah Yahusha ^(replaced with Yeshua/Jesus).
Gal. 3:27 F or as many as were baptized into Messiah, you put on Messiah.
Gal. 3:28 There cannot be Jew nor Greek, there is no slave nor free-man, there is no male and female; for you are all one in Messiah Yahusha ^(replaced with Yeshua/Jesus).
Gal. 3:29 And if you *are* of Messiah, then you are a seed of Abraham, even heirs according to promise.

All Have Sinned In the Fathers Eyes

Psa. 143:2 and do not enter into judgment with your servant for not anyone living is just in Your sight

Psa. 14:1 *To the chief musician. A Psalm of David.* The fool has said in his heart, *There is* no Elohim ^{(Mighty one(s)/God)}! They acted corruptly; they did hatefully in deeds; there is none doing good.
Psa. 14:2 Yahuah ^(Replaced with Lord/God) looked down from Heaven on the sons of mankind, to see if there were any discerning *and* seeking Elohim ^{(Mighty one(s)/God)}:
Psa. 14:3 they *have* all turned aside; together they have become filthy; *there is* none doing good, not even one!

Isa. 64:6 But we are all as the unclean *thing*, and all our righteousness *are* as a menstruation cloth. And we all fade as a leaf, and like the wind our iniquities take us away.

Rom. 3:12 All turned away, *they* became worthless together, not *one is* doing goodness, not so much as one! *LXX-Psa. 13:1-3*
Rom. 3:13 "Their throat *is* a tomb being opened;" "they used deceit with their tongues; *the* poison of asps *is* under their lips;
Rom. 3:14 whose mouth *is* full of cursing and bitterness.
Rom. 3:15 Their feet *are* swift to shed blood;
Rom. 3:16 ruin and misery *are* in their way;
Rom. 3:17 and they did not know a way of peace;
Rom. 3:18 there is no fear of Elohim ^{(Mighty one(s)/God)} before their eyes."
LXX-Psa. 5:10; 139:4; 9:28; Isa. 59:7, 8; Psa. 35:2; MT -Psa. 14:1-3; 5:9; 140:3; 10:7; Isa. 59:7, 8; Psa. 36:1
Rom. 3:19 But we know that whatever the Law says, it speaks to those within the Law, so that every mouth may be stopped, and all the world be under judgment to Elohim ^{(Mighty one(s)/God)}.
Rom. 3:20 Because by works of Law not one of all flesh will be justified before Him, for through Law *is* full knowledge of sin. *Psa. 143:2*
Rom. 3:21 But now a righteousness of Elohim ^{(Mighty one(s)/God)} has been revealed apart from Law, being witnessed by the Law and the Prophets,
Rom. 3:22 even the righteousness of Elohim ^{(Mighty one(s)/God)} through faith of Yahusha ^(replaced with Yeshua/Jesus) Messiah toward all and upon all those believing; for there is no difference,
Rom. 3:23 for all sinned and fall short of the glory of Elohim ^{(Mighty one(s)/God)},
Rom. 3:24 being justified freely by His favor through the redemption in Messiah Yahusha ^(replaced with Yeshua/Jesus),
Rom. 3:25 whom Elohim ^{(Mighty one(s)/God)} set forth *as* a propitiation through faith in His blood, as a demonstration of His righteousness through the passing over of the sins that had taken place before, in the forbearance of Elohim ^{(Mighty one(s)/God)},
Rom. 3:26 for a demonstration of His righteousness in the present time, for His being just and justifying the *one* that *is* of the faith of Yahusha ^(replaced with Yeshua/Jesus).
Rom. 3:27 Then where *is* the boasting? It was excluded. Through what law? Of works? No, but through a Law of faith.

Rom. 3:28 Then we conclude a man to be justified by faith without works of Law.

Rom. 3:29 Or *is He* the Elohim ^{(Mighty one(s)/God)} of Jews only, and not also of the nations? Yes of the nations also,

Rom. 3:30 since *it is* one Elohim ^{(Mighty one(s)/God)} who will justify circumcision by faith, and un-circumcision through faith.

Rom. 3:31 Then *is* the Law annulled through faith? Let it not be! But we establish Law.

Paul urges Believers to imitate Him

1Co. 4:15 For if you should have myriads of **teachers** in Messiah, yet not many fathers; for I fathered you in Messiah Yahusha ^(replaced with Yeshua/Jesus) through the good news.

1Co. 4:16 Because of this, I urge you, be **imitators** of me.

1Co. 4:17 Because of this I sent Timothy to you, who is my beloved child, and faithful in Yahuah ^(Replaced with Lord/God), who will remind you *of* my ways in Messiah, even as I teach everywhere in every assembly.

The Law is Our Schoolmaster before Messiah came. Let's See what this letter is all about.

G3807 ¹αιδαγωγος paidagogos

Thayer Definition:

1) a tutor, i.e. a guardian and guide of boys.

Among the Greeks and the Romans this name was applied to trustworthy servants who were charged with the duty of supervising the life and morals of boys belonging to the better class. The boys were not allowed so much as to step out of the house without them before arriving at the age of manhood.

This word is used else where in 1Cor. 4:15

1Co 4:15 For if you should have myriads of **teachers (attendant)** in Messiah, yet not many fathers; for I fathered you in Messiah Yahusha ^(replaced with Yeshua/Jesus) through the good news.

In Galatians the fourth Chapter, Paul cannot be saying the Law is the schoolmaster because the schoolmaster is the attendant to the child while he is a servant and in bondage to the elements of the world. The Law does not bring one into bondage. The law that is a schoolmaster must be referring to religious law, or secular law that kept us shut up until we came to faith...if we had already came to faith we would be following the Law. A person who doesn't have faith does not follow the Law, this makes no sense.

Another hint that **paidagogos** is not referring to the Law is the fact that this word is used in the **Septuagint one time, and in Macc. 1:10**.

The word paidagogos is connected with another Greek word usually translated as teacher or master. The idea of the rab-bis/religious leaders as schoolmasters certainly fits the context of Scripture better than the Law being a schoolmaster
Didaskolos from the Theological Dictionary of the New Testament (→ rhabb.).
A. The Usage and Character of didskalos among the Greeks.
1. The Usage. This word is attested from the Homeric hymns, the feminine also occurring. It means "instructor" as
a. "schoolmaster"
b. **In contrast Epictetus is proud to be called a didskalos, for as the teacher of a system he is helping to bring his followers to perfection** (Dissertationes 1.9.12).
c. The LXX has didskalos only in Esth. 6:1 and 2 Macc. 1:10. In Esther the use is the regular Greek one, but in Maccabees Aristobulus is called didskalos as an expositor of the law, so that the word has a special meaning (parallel to didskōn) **as one who gives direction in the way of Elohim** (Mighty one(s)/God). **The general use for paid or official teachers worked against its more widespread adoption in this sense**.

The didskaloi of the Early believer's Community.

a. The references to believer's, didskaloi in Acts and the epistles are in keeping with the Hebraic usage. Thus in Jms. 3:1, especially if the letter is early or derives from rabbinic Judaism, the meaning is the expositor of the law who makes a right fulfillment possible.

From Vines Dictionary of New Testament words:
<A-1,Noun,1320,*didaskalos*> "a teacher" (from didasko, "to teach"), is frequently rendered "Master" in the four Gospels, as a title of address to Messiah,
e.g., Mat 8:19; Mar 4:38 (there are more instances in Luke than in the other Gospels); Joh 1:38, where it interprets "Rabbi;" Joh 20:16, where it interprets "Rabboni." It is used by Messiah of Himself in Mat 23:8 (see No. 6) and Joh 13:13-14; by others concerning Him, Mat 17:24; Mat 26:18; Mar 5:35; Mar 14:14; Luk 8:49; Luk 22:11; Joh 11:28. In Joh 3:10, Yahuah ^(Replaced with Lord/God) uses it in addressing Nicodemus, RV, "the teacher" (AV , "a master"), where the article does not specify a particular "teacher," but designates the member of a class; for the class see Luk 2:46, "the doctors" (RV , marg., "teachers"). It is used of the relation of a disciple to his "master," in Mat 10:24-25; Luk 6:40. It is not translated "masters" in the rest of the NT, save in the AV of Jam 3:1 "(be not many) masters," where obviously the RV "teachers" is the meaning. See TEACHER.
We are no longer under a schoolmaster "Law", meaning we are not to follow the Law by our fleshly strength. We are to Follow the Spirit that leads and guide us to all truth. As was stated earlier, His Commandments and Law is Truth. Another way of saying this, is the Spirit of the Law. The Law was not designed to give you Salvation, but to lead you to Salvation. It also teaches you how to treat one another, and How the Most High wants to be treated. When you are "Under the Law" you are subject to the curses and death of it, If you BREAK IT. The Messiah came not to do away with the Laws or the Prophets *Matt. 5:17*, but give us a chance and repent from breaking the Laws so that we would not suffer any curses or Death. For the wages of Sin is DEATH. SIN is transgression of the LAW. Let's look at a quick example:

- **John 8:3** And the scribes and Pharisees brought unto him a woman taken in adultery; and when they had set her in the midst,

  John 8:4 They say unto him, Teacher, this woman was taken in adultery, in the very Acts.

  John 8:5 Now Moses in the law commanded us, that such should be stoned: but what say you?

John 8:6 This they said, tempting him, that they might have to accuse him. But Yahusha ^(replaced with Yeshua/Jesus) stooped down, and with *his* finger wrote on the ground, *as though he heard them not.*

John 8:7 So when they continued asking him, he lifted up himself, and said unto them, He that is without sin among you, let him first cast a stone at her.

John 8:8 And again he stooped down, and wrote on the ground.

John 8.9 And they which heard *it*, being convicted by *their own* conscience, went out one by one, beginning at the eldest, *even* unto the last: and Yahusha ^(replaced with Yeshua/Jesus) was left alone, and the woman standing in the midst.

John 8:10 When Yahusha ^(replaced with Yeshua/Jesus) had lifted up himself, and saw none but the woman, he said unto her, Woman, where are those your accusers? have no man condemned you?

John 8:11 She said, No man, Sovereign. And Yahusha ^(replaced with Yeshua/Jesus) said unto her, <u>**Neither do I condemn you: go, and sin no more.**</u>

What you should have drawn from this story is She was suppose to have been stoned or death was to take place, but the Messiah did not condemn her. A better way of saying this, was He gave her Grace. Then said SIN NO MORE. Meaning, do not violate the Law.

- o [Noteworthy, the Man whom she committed adultery was suppose to be there with her, so that they stone him as well. But you can see how the Scribes and Pharisees, transgressed the Law, by their traditions].

Rom. 6:14 For your sin shall not sovereign over you, for you are not under Law, but under favor.

Rom. 6:15 What then? **Shall we sin because we are not under Law, but under favor? Let it not be!**

Rom. 6:16 Do you not know that to whom you present yourselves *as* slaves for obedience, you are slaves to whom you obey, whether of **sin to death**, OR **obedience to righteousness**?

Rom. 6:17 But thanks *be* to Elohim ^{(Mighty one(s)/God)} that you were servants of sin, but you obeyed from *the* heart the form of doctrine to which you were delivered.

Rom. 6:18 And having been **set free from sin**, you were enslaved to righteousness.

We Walk by Faith, Does That Mean We Stop Following The Law?

Rom. 2:13 For not the hearers of the Law are just with Elohim ^{(Mighty one(s)/God)}, but **the doers of the Law shall be justified**.

Rom. 2:14 For when nations not having Law do by nature the things of the Law, they not having Law are a law to themselves,

Rom. 2:15 who **show the work of the Law written in their hearts**, their conscience witnessing with *them*, and the thoughts between one another accusing or even excusing,

We can follow the Law without even knowing the letter, we can also know the letter of the law but not follow it.

Rom. 2:26 If, then, the un-circumcision keeps the ordinances of the Law, *will* not his un-circumcision be counted for circumcision?

Rom. 2:27 And will *not* the un-circumcision by nature *by* completing the Law judge you, **the *one who* through letter and circumcision** *becomes* **transgressor of Law?**

Rom. 2:28 For he is not a Jew that *is one* outwardly, nor *is* circumcision that outwardly in flesh;

Rom. 2:29 **but he *is* a Jew that *is one* inwardly, and circumcision *is* of heart, in spirit, not in letter; of whom the praise *is* not from men, but from Elohim** ^{(Mighty one(s)/God)}.

When we receive the Holy Spirit, we don't need the letter of the law anymore. The Spirit tells us the way in which we should walk. And it would not be contrary to the Law.

- **Isa. 30:21** And your ears shall hear a word behind you, saying, **This is the way, walk in it** when you go right or when you go left.

- **Deut. 5:32 And you shall be careful to do as Yahuah** ^(Replaced with Lord/God) **your Elohim** ^{(Mighty one(s)/God)} **has commanded you; you shall not turn aside to the right or left.**
- Deut. 5:33 **You shall walk in all the ways** which Yahuah ^{(Re-}

79

placed with Lord/God) your Elohim (Mighty one(s)/God) has commanded
you, so that you may live, and *that* good *may be* to you, and
you may prolong *your* days in the land which you will possess.

The problem is that the lawlessness of this world brands our hearts so
that we think there are certain or all commandments that don't apply to
us anymore or that certain or all commandments are done away with or
fulfilled or nailed to the cross etc etc etc.....

- **Matt. 24:11** And many false prophets will be raised and will
  cause many to err.
  Matt. 24:12 And because lawlessness shall have been multi-
  plied, the love of the many will grow cold.

- **1Ti. 4:2** Speaking lies in hypocrisy; having their **conscience
  seared with a hot iron**;
    o   When our conscience is seared it becomes dull and
        without feeling

- **Isa. 6:9** And He said, Go and say to this people, Hearing you
  hear, but do not understand; and seeing you see, but do not
  know.
  Isa 6:10 Make the heart of this people fat, and make his ears
  heavy, and shut his eyes, that he not see with his eyes, and hear
  with his ears and understand with his heart and turn back, and
  one heals him. What is a hard heart?

- **Zech. 7:11** But they refused to listen, and gave a stubborn
  shoulder, and they made their ears heavy from hearing.
  Zech 7:12 And **they made their heart adamant from hearing
  the Law** and the Words which Yahuah (Replaced with Lord/God) of
  Hosts has sent by the former prophets through His Spirit. And
  great wrath was from Yahuah (Replaced with Lord/God) of Hosts.

  Heb. 5:8 though being a Son, He learned obedience from what
  He suffered
  Heb. 5:9 and having been perfected, He came to be *the* Author
  of eternal salvation to all the *ones* obeying Him,
  Heb. 5:10 having been called out by Elohim (Mighty one(s)/God) *as* a

80

High Priest according to the order of Melchizedek.
Heb. 5:11 Concerning whom we *have* much discourse, and hard to interpret, *or* to speak, since you have come to be dull in the hearings.

This is why many twist Paul's writings

2Pe. 3:15 And think of the long-suffering of our Sovereign *as* salvation, as also our beloved brother Paul wrote to you, according to the wisdom given to him;
2Pe. 3:16 as also in all his epistles, speaking in them concerning these things, **in which are some things hard to understand,** which the unlearned and unsettled pervert as also *they do* the rest of the Scriptures to *their* own destruction.
2Pe. 3:17 Then beloved, you knowing beforehand, **watch lest being led away by the error of the lawless** you fall from *your* own steadfastness.

Peter was addressing something that was so prevalent, even today. People twisted Paul's Letters because they were and are hard at times to understand. Since they are hard to understand they also pervert the scriptures as verse 16 states. Have you taken any note that Peter does not call Paul's epistle Scripture; and that people were using Paul's letters to pervert scripture? What should come to mind is what is scripture. *See Luke 24:44-45*
We have grown cold, hard, and dull of hearing. This is why most believe that the law does not apply to them and why many when their eyes are opened and begin to keep the law stop walking in the spirit and start trying to follow the Law by THEIR strength. Those who keep the law can often forget to listen to the Spirit.

We stop listening to that still, small voice.

1Ki. 19:11 And he said, Go out and stand on the mountain before Yahuah ^(Replaced with Lord/God). And, behold, Yahuah ^(Replaced with Lord/God) passed by, and a great and strong wind tearing the mountains and breaking the rocks in bits before Yahuah ^(Replaced with Lord/God)! Yahuah ^(Replaced with Lord/God) *was* not in the wind.
And after the wind *was* an earthquake, *but* Yahuah ^(Replaced with Lord/God)

was not in the earthquake.

1Ki. 19:12 And after the earthquake *was* a fire, *but* Yahuah [Replaced with Lord/God] *was* not in the fire; and after the fire *came* a still small voice.

2 Esdras 3:19 And your glory went through four gates, of fire, and of earthquake, and of wind, and of cold; that you might give the law unto the seed of Jacob, and diligence unto the generation of Israel.

2 Esdras 3:20 And yet took you not away from them a wicked heart, that your law might bring forth fruit in them.

John Gill's commentary
and after the fire a still small voice: not rough, but gentle, more like whispering than roaring; something soft, easy, and musical; the Targum is, the voice of those that praise Elohim [Mighty one(s)/God] in silence; and all this may be considered as showing the difference between the two dispensations of law and Good news; the law is a voice of terrible words, and was given amidst a tempest of wind, thunder, and lightning, attended with an earthquake, Heb. 12:18, but the Good news is a gentle voice of love, favor, and mercy, of peace, pardon, righteousness, and salvation by Messiah; and may also point at the order and manner of Yahuah's [Replaced with Lord/God] dealings with the souls of men, who usually by the law breaks the rocky hearts of men in pieces, shakes their consciences, and fills their minds with a sense of fiery wrath and indignation they deserve, and then speaks comfortably to them, speaks peace and pardon through the ministration of the Good news by his Spirit; blessed are the people that hear this still, small, gentle voice, the joyful sound, Psa. 89:15.

John Wesley's commentary
1Ki. 19:12 - A still voice - To intimate, that Elohim [Mighty one(s)/God] would do his work in and for Israel in his own time, not by might or power, but by his own spirit, Zech. 4:6, which moves with a powerful, but yet with a sweet and gentle gale.

Zech. 4:6 Then he answered and spoke to me, saying, This *is* the Word of Yahuah [Replaced with Lord/God] to Zerubbabel saying, **Not by might, nor by power, but by My Spirit, says Yahuah** [Replaced with Lord/God] **of Hosts.**

Pro. 3:1 My son, do not forget my law, but let your heart keep my

commands,

Pro. 3:2 for they shall add length of days and long life and peace to you.

Pro. 3:3 Mercy and truth will not forsake you, tie them on your neck, **write them on the tablet of your heart** (^{re}new covenant),

Pro. 3:4 and you shall find favor & good understanding in the sight of Elohim ^{(Mighty one(s)/God)} and man.

Pro. 3:5 **Trust in Yahuah** ^(Replaced with Lord/God) **with all your heart, and lean not to your own understanding**.

Pro. 3:6 **In all your ways acknowledge Him, and He shall direct your paths**. (Follow His Spirit, He will lead you in the way you should go)

Pro. 3:7 Do not be wise in your own eyes fear Yahuah ^(Replaced with Lord/God) and depart from evil

CHAPTER 4

Gal. 4:1 But I say, over so long a time the heir is an infant he being sovereign of all does not differ from a servant,

Could this be a reference to Ezekiel? Though Israel is His Son, yet they were born in slavery to the World.

Ezek. 16:1 And the Word of Yahuah ^(Replaced with Lord/God) came to me, saying,

Ezek. 16:2 Son of man, cause Jerusalem to know her abominations,

Ezek. 16:3 and say, So says Sovereign Yahuah ^(Replaced with Lord/God) to Jerusalem: Your origin and your birth *is* of the land of Canaan. Your father *was* an Amorite and your mother a Hittite.

Ezek. 16:4 *As for* your birth, in the day you were born, your navel was not cut and you were not washed with water to cleanse *you*. And you were not salted, and you *were* not at all swaddled.

Ezek. 16:5 An eye did not have pity on you to do to you one of these, to have compassion on you. But you were thrown into the face of the field, for your person *was* loathed in the day you were born.

Ezek. 16:6 And *when* I passed by you and saw you squirming in your blood, I said to you in your blood, Live Yea, I said to you in your blood, Live!

Ezek. 16:7 As a myriad, as a field shoot I have given you, and you are grown and are great And you come *in* the finest ornaments. *Your* breasts are formed, and *your* hair is grown, yet you *were* naked and bare.

Ezek. 16:8 And I passed by you, and I looked on you, and, behold, your time *was* the time of love. And I spread My skirt over you and covered your nakedness. And I swore to you and entered into a covenant with you, declares Sovereign Yahuah ^(Replaced with Lord/God). And you became Mine.

Ezek. 16:9 And I washed you with water; I washed away your blood from you, and I anointed you with oil.

Ezek. 16:10 And I dressed you *with* embroidered work, and I shod you *with* dugong *sandals*. And I wrapped you in fine linen, and I covered you *with* silk.

Ezek. 16:11 And I adorned you *with* ornaments, and I put bracelets on your hands and a chain on your neck.

Ezek. 16:12 And I put a ring on your nose and earrings on your ears and a crown of beauty on your head.

Ezek. 16:13 And you were adorned with gold and silver. And your clothing *was* fine linen and silk and embroidered work. Fine flour and honey and oil you ate. And you were very, very beautiful And you advanced to regal estate.

Ezek. 16:14 And your name went out among the nations, because of your beauty, for it *was* perfect by My splendor which I had set on you, declares Sovereign Yahuah ^(Replaced with Lord/God).

Ezek. 16:15 But you trusted in your beauty, and *you* prostituted *yourself* because of your name, and poured out your fornications on all who passed by; it was to him!

Gal. 4:2 but is under **guardians** and **housemasters** until the *term* set before by the father.

Gal. 4:3 So we also, when we were infants, we were under the **elements of the world, being enslaved.**

Hos. 4:6 My people are cut off for lack of knowledge. Because you rejected the knowledge, I also rejected you from being priest to Me. Since you have forgotten the Law of your Elohim ^{(Mighty one(s)/God)}, I will forget your son's even. I Israel became slaves to the elements of the world and statutes and judgments that were not good for us.

Gal. 4:4 But when the fullness of the time came, Elohim ^{(Mighty one(s)/God)}

sent forth His Son, having come into being out of a woman, having come under Law,

Gal. 4:5 that He might redeem the ones under Law, **that we might receive the adoption of sons**.

Israel were enslaved due to disobedience

Deut. 24:18 But you shall remember that you were a slave in Egypt and Yahuah ^(Replaced with Lord/God) your Elohim ^{(Mighty one(s)/God)} redeemed you from there. For that reason I command you to do this thing.

Jer. 17:4 And you, even through yourself, will let drop from your inheritance which I gave you. And I will cause you to serve your enemies in a land that you do not know. For you have kindled a fire in My anger; it will burn forever.

Lam. 5:1 O Yahuah ^(Replaced with Lord/God), remember what has been to us; look upon and see our reproach.
Lam. 5:2 Our inheritance has been turned to aliens, our houses to foreigners.
Lam. 5:3 We are orphans *There is* no father our mothers *are* like widows
Lam. 5:4 We have drunk our water for silver our wood comes for a price.
Lam 5:5 We *are* pursued; we grow weary; rest is not given to us
Lam. 5:6 We have given the hand *to* the Egyptian's to the Assyrian, in order to be satisfied with bread.
Lam. 5:7 Our fathers have sinned, and *are* not we have borne their iniquities.
Lam. 5:8 Slaves rule over us; *there is* no rescuer from their hand.

Ezek. 20:23 And I lifted up My hand to them in the wilderness, to scatter them among the nations and sow them among the lands,
Ezek. 20:24 because they had not done My judgments and had despised My statutes and had profaned My Sabbaths. And their eyes were after their fathers' idols.
Ezek. 20:25 Therefore I also gave them statutes *that were* not good, and judgments by *which* they could not live.

Gal. 4:7 So that you no more are a slave, but a son, and if a son, also an heir of Elohim ^{(Mighty one(s)/God)} through Messiah.
Yahuah ^(Replaced with Lord/God) brought us out of Slavery to follow His Law. Did the Creator take Israel out of bondage to put them in bondage using the Law?

Jer. 11:2 Hear the Words of this covenant, and speak to the men of Judah, and to those living in Jerusalem,
Jer. 11:3 and say to them, So says Yahuah ^(Replaced with Lord/God), the Elohim ^{(Mighty one(s)/God)} of Israel, Cursed is the man who does not obey the Words of this covenant,
Jer. 11:4 which I commanded your fathers in the day I brought them out of the land of Egypt, from the iron furnace, saying, Obey My voice and do them according to all that I command you, so that you shall be My people, and I will be your Elohim ^{(Mighty one(s)/God)};
Jer. 11:5 in order to establish the oath which I swore to your fathers, to give them a land flowing with milk and honey, as it is this day. Then I answered and said, Amen, O Yahuah ^(Replaced with Lord/God).
Jer. 11:6 And Yahuah ^(Replaced with Lord/God) said to me, Declare all these Words in the cities of Judah, and in the streets of Jerusalem, saying, Hear the Words of this covenant and do them.

Gal. 4:8 But then, indeed, not knowing Elohim ^{(Mighty one(s)/God)}, you served as slaves to the ones by nature not being gods.

Slaves to the Elements of the World, because Israel turned from Elohim ^{(Mighty one(s)/God)}

Isa. 63:16 For You are our Father, though Abraham does not know us, and Israel does not acknowledge us; You, Yahuah ^(Replaced with Lord/God), are our Father, our Redeemer; Your name is from everlasting.
Isa. 63:17 O Yahuah ^(Replaced with Lord/God), why do You make us wander from Your ways? You harden our heart from Your fear. For Your servants' sake, return the tribes of Your inheritance.
Isa. 63:18 For a little while Your Holy people possessed it. Our enemies have trampled Your sanctuary.
Isa. 63:19 We are of old; You never ruled over them. Your name was never called on them.

Acts 14:11 And seeing what Paul did, the crowd lifted up their voice in Lycaonian, saying, The gods have come down to us, becoming like men.

1Co. 10:20 But the things the nations sacrifice, "they sacrifice to demons, and not to Elohim ^{(Mighty one(s)/God)}." *Deut. 32:17* But I do not want you to become sharers of demons;

Gal. 4:9 But now, knowing Elohim ^{(Mighty one(s)/God)}, but rather being known by Elohim ^{(Mighty one(s)/God)}, how do you turn again to the weak and poor elements to which you desire again to slave anew?

Is Paul telling the Galatians not to follow the Law because it is weak and would enslave them? If verse 8 is true, which states the Galatians did not know Elohim ^{(Mighty one(s)/God)}, would they have been following Law?

Col. 2:8 Watch that there not be one robbing you through philosophy and empty deceit, according to the tradition of men, according to the elements of the world, and not according to Messiah.

Col. 2:20 If, then, you died with Messiah from the elements of the world, why are you under its decrees, as living in the world?
Col. 2:21 Do not handle, do not taste, do not touch,
Col. 2:22 which things are all for corruption in the using, according to the
"injunctions and teachings of men." *Isa. 29:13*

Gal. 4:10 You observe days and months and seasons and years.
- THIS IS TALKING ABOUT THE BIBLICAL FEASTS RIGHT?
  ABSOLUTELY NOT!

Deut. 18:10 There shall not be found among you any one that makes his son or his daughter to pass through the fire, or that use divination, or an observer of times, or an enchanter, or a witch,

Lev. 19:26 You shall not eat any thing with the blood: neither shall you use   enchantment, nor observe times.

Note: Gal.4:9 states that they did not know Elohim so they could not be observing His days and months and seasons and years. A good search would reveal that these days and months and seasons and years were to a pagan deity.

Gal. 4:21 Tell me, those desiring to be under Law, do you not hear the Law?

.

Rom. 2:12 For as many as sinned without Law will also perish without Law. And as many as sinned within Law will be judged through Law.

What the letter to the Galatians is telling them is to listen to what the Law is saying. To do that one must learn and understand the Law. When one goes back to hear the law (which is what we have been doing this whole time) one will see that the law is divided into two categories, blessings and curses. The blessings not the curses are what is desired. When one sins or transgresses the law, however, curses are inherited. It is for this reason that the Messiah died, that we might no longer have to pay the penalty for breaking the law or our sins, which brought curses and death. So the Messiah did not die to take away the law but rather the judgment of its violation. Thus, giving us the opportunity to repent and receive His blessings and life.

So many times we read in scripture how they violated the law then tried to fix it through works of law. They became a slave to the law in that they could sin as much as they liked and all they had to do was make a sacrifice and be forgiven. So how did Messiah put a stop to this willful or intentional disobedience. *Hebrews 10:26-27*

Gal. 3:10 For as many as are out of works of Law, these are under a curse. For it   has been written, "Cursed is everyone who does not continue in all the things having been written in the book of the Law, to do them." *Deut. 27:26*

Gal. 4:22 For it has been written, Abraham had two sons, one out of the slave woman and one out of the free woman.

- **Rom. 9:8** That is: Not the children of flesh are children of Elohim ^{(Mighty one(s)/God)}, but the children of the promise are counted for a seed.

88

Gal. 4:23 But, indeed, he of the slave woman has been born according to flesh, and he out of the free woman through the promise,

- **Rom. 9:31** but Israel following after a Law of righteousness did not arrive at a Law of righteousness?
  Rom. 9:32 Why? Because it was not of faith, but as of works of Law. For they stumbled at the Stone-of-stumbling,

What Paul is explaining here is righteousness by works or righteousness by faith.

Abraham tried to bring about the Promise of Yahuah (Replaced with Lord/God) *by going into Hagar, which brought forth Ishmael, This is righteousness by works. But Yahuah* (Replaced with Lord/God) *said the heir would be Isaac, who is righteousness by Faith.*

Gal. 4:24 which things are being allegorized, for these are two covenants, one, indeed, from Mount Sinai bringing forth to slavery (which is Hagar,
Gal. 4:25 for Hagar is Mount Sinai in Arabia and corresponds to the present Jerusalem, and she slaves with her children),
Gal. 4:26 but the Jerusalem from above is free, who is the mother of us all;
Gal. 4:27 for it has been written, "Be glad, barren one not bearing; break forth and shout, the one not travailing; for more are the children of the desolate rather than she having the husband." *Isa. 54:1*
Gal. 4:28 But, brothers, we are children of promise according to Isaac.

The parallel in this allegorical statement is showing how Hagar was the slave, which represents going to Mount Sinai without Faith. When you go back and read the story, you will find that Abraham and Sarah tried to make the promise come to past through there way and not The Father's way. In essences without faith trying to do the Law would put you in bondage. The promise was with Isaac, But He was still subject to the law, just Faith and promises was given to and through him. Another way of comparing the two is Ishmael/works/religion & Isaac/faith/Word.

Laughter is also associated with being freed/loosed from bondage when we are restored from our captivity.

Psa. 126:1 A Song of Ascents. When Yahuah ^(Replaced with Lord/God) turned back the captivity of Zion, we were like those who dream.
Psa. 126:2 Then our mouth was full of laughter, and our tongue with joyful shouting; then they said among the nations, Yahuah ^(Replaced with Lord/God) will work great things with these.

In Galatians Four Paul is making word play on the meaning of the word freedom. This is freedom from sin and bondage that brings us into the family of Elohim ^{(Mighty one(s)/God)}.

1Ma. 2:8 Her temple is become as a man without glory.
1Ma. 2:9 Her esteemed vessels are carried away into captivity, her infants are slain in the streets, her young men with the sword of the enemy.
1Ma. 2:10 What nation has not had a part in her kingdom and gotten of her spoils?
1Ma. 2:11 All her ornaments are taken away of a free woman she is become a bond-slave.

Does Law bring us into Bondage?

Joh. 8:32 And you will know the truth, and the truth will set you free.

Psa. 119:142 Your righteousness is forever, and Your Law is truth.

Psa. 119:45 And I will walk in a wide space ^(LIBERTY), for I seek Your Commands.

Jas. 1:25 But the one looking into the perfect Law of liberty, and continuing in it, this one not having become a forgetful hearer, but a doer of the work, this one will be blessed in his doing.

Rom. 8:21 that also the creation will be freed from the slavery of corruption to the freedom of the glory of the children of Elohim ^{(Mighty one(s)/God)}.

Rev 22:3 And every curse will no longer be. And the throne of Elohim [Mighty one(s)/God] and the Lamb will be in it; and His servants will serve Him.

Isa. 66:22 For as the new heavens and the new earth that I make stand before Me, declares Yahuah [Replaced with Lord/God], so your seed and your name shall stand.
Isa. 66:23 And it will be, from new moon to its new moon, and from Sabbath to its Sabbath, all flesh shall come to worship before Me, says Yahuah [Replaced with Lord/God].

2Pe. 3:13 But according to His promise, we look for "new heavens and a new earth," in which righteousness dwells. *Isa. 65:17*

Rev. 21:27 And all profaning may not at all enter into it, or any making an abomination or a lie; but only the ones having been written in the Book of Life of the Lamb.

Gal. 4:28 But, brothers, we are children of promise according to Isaac.
Gal. 4:29 But then, even as he born according to flesh persecuted the one according to Spirit, so it is also now.

Spiritual verses Fleshly

Rom. 8:7 because the mind of the flesh is enmity towards Elohim [Mighty one(s)/God]; for it is not being subjected to the Law of Elohim [Mighty one(s)/God], for neither can it be
Rom. 8:8 And those being in the flesh are not able to please Elohim [Mighty one(s)/God].

Rom. 7:14 For we know that the Law is spiritual, but I am fleshly, having been sold under sin.

Gal. 4:31 Then, brothers, we are not children of a slave woman but of the free woman.

- Rom. 6:16 Do you not know that to whom you present yourselves as slaves for obedience, you are slaves to whom you obey, whether of sin to death, or obedience to righteousness?

Rom. 6:17 But thanks be to Elohim ^{(Mighty one(s)/God)} that you were slaves of sin, but you obeyed from the heart the form of doctrine to which you were delivered.

Rom 6:18 And having been set free from sin, you were enslaved to righteousness.

CHAPTER 5

Gal. 5:1 Then stand firm in the freedom with which Messiah made us free and do not be held again with a yoke of slavery.
So is this saying we are freed from the "Old Testament" which is suppose to bring Bondage?

Rom. 8:21 that also the creation will be freed from the slavery of corruption to the freedom of the glory of the children of Elohim ^{(Mighty one(s)/God)}.

Heb. 2:14 Since, then, the children have partaken of flesh and blood, in like manner He Himself also shared the same things, that through death He might cause to cease the one having the power of death, that is, the devil;

Heb. 2:15 and might set these free, as many as by fear of death were subject to slavery through all the lifetime to live.

Psa. 119:45 And I will walk in liberty: for I seek your precepts.

Matt. 11:28 Come to Me, all those laboring and being burdened, and I will give you rest.

Matt. 11:29 Take My yoke upon you and learn from Me, because I am meek and lowly in heart, "and you will find rest to your souls." *Jer. 6:16*

Matt. 11:30 For My yoke is easy, and My burden is light.

Luk. 16:17 But it is easier for the heaven and the earth to pass away than one point of the Law to fail.

Gal. 5:2 Behold, I, Paul, say to you that if you are circumcised, Messiah will profit you nothing.

Gal. 5:3 And I witness again to every man being circumcised, that he

is a debtor to do all the Law,
Gal. 5:4 you whoever are justified by Law, you were severed from Messiah; you fell from favor.

Is it wrong or was Paul saying it was wrong to circumcise, if we keep the Law, we have fallen from Grace? What Paul is saying, if you try to keep the Law in order to be justified by it, then you have fallen from Grace because you are denting the gift of forgiveness and salvation through the Messiah Circumcision which is a perpetual covenant, that came before the Mount Sinai covenant.

- Gen. 17:13 The child of your house and the purchase of your money circumcising must be circumcised. And My covenant shall be in your flesh for a perpetual covenant.
- (Keep in mind We are of Abraham's seed, which we read earlier in Chapter 3).

The scriptures states when the Kingdom is rebuilt here on earth, circumcision we still be taking place.

Ezek. 44:9 So says Sovereign Yahuah ^(Replaced with Lord/God): No son of an alien, uncircumcised of heart and uncircumcised of flesh, shall enter into My sanctuary, or any son of an alien who is among the sons of Israel.

Isa. 52:1 Awake! Awake! Put on your strength, Zion; put on your beautiful robes, O Jerusalem, the Holy city. For never again shall uncircumcised and unclean ones come to you.

If circumcision was done away, why would Paul circumcise Timothy?
- Acts 16:1 And he arrived in Derbe and Lystra. And behold, a certain disciple named Timothy was there, the son of a certain believing Jewish woman, but his father was a Greek.
  Acts 16:2 This one was being witnessed of by the brothers in Lystra and Iconium.
  Acts 16:3 Paul desired this one to go forth with him, and taking him he circumcised him, because of the Jews being in those places. For they all knew his father, that he was a Greek.

I believe Paul was trying to put the priorities of the Galatians back in

Rom. 7:12 So indeed the Law is Holy, and the commandment Holy and just and good.

Rom. 7:13 Then that which is good, has it become death to me? Let it not be! But sin, that it might appear to be sin, having worked out death to me through the good, in order that sin might become excessively sinful through the commandment.

Rom. 7:14 For we know that the Law is spiritual, but I am fleshly, having been sold under sin.

Rom. 7:15 For what I work out, I do not know. For what I do not will, this I do. But what I hate, this I do.

Rom. 7:16 But if I do what I do not will, I agree with the Law, that it is good.

Rom. 7:17 But now I no longer work it out, but the sin dwelling in me.

Rom. 7:18 For I know that in me, that is in my flesh, dwells no good. For to will is present to me, but to work out the good I do not find.

Rom. 7:19 For what good I desire, I do not do. But the evil I do not desire, this I do.

Rom. 7:20 But if I do what I do not desire, it is no longer I working it out, but the sin dwelling in me.

Rom. 7:21 I find then the Law, when I desire to do the right, that evil is present with me.

Rom. 7:22 For I delight in the Law of Elohim (Mighty one(s)/God) according to the inward man;

Rom. 7:23 but I see another Law in my members having warred against the Law of my mind, and taking me captive by the Law of sin being in my members.

Rom. 7:24 O wretched man that I am! Who shall deliver me from the body of this death?

Rom. 7:25 I thank Elohim (Mighty one(s)/God) through Yahusha (replaced with Yeshua/Jesus) Messiah our sovereign! So then I myself with the mind truly serve the Law of Elohim (Mighty one(s)/God), and with the flesh the law of sin.

Not under the law means:

1) No longer under the penalty of the Law which is the curse because of disobedience.

2) No longer follow only the letter of the law but we are to follow the Holy spirit which if we do, we will not only fulfill the letter of the law but also the spirit of the law. This is simplified by saying walk in love.

CHAPTER 6

Gal. 6:12 As many as desire to look well in the flesh, these compel you to be circumcised, only that they may not be persecuted for the cross of Messiah.

Gal. 6:13 For they themselves having been circumcised do not even keep the Law, but they desire you to be circumcised so that they may boast in your flesh.

Gal. 6:14 But may it never be for me to boast, except in the stake of our Sovereign Yahusha ^(replaced with Yeshua/Jesus) Messiah, through whom the world has been crucified to me, and I to the world.

Gal. 6:15 For in Messiah Yahusha ^(replaced with Yeshua/Jesus) neither circumcision has any strength nor un-circumcision, but a new creation.

Gal. 6:16 And as many as shall walk by this rule, peace and mercy be on them and on the Israel of Elohim ^(Mighty one(s)/God).

HARD SAYINGS OF PAUL

2Pe. 3:14 Wherefore, beloved, seeing that you look for such things, be diligent that you may be found of him in peace, without spot, and blameless.

2Pe. 3:15 And account *that* the longsuffering of our Sovereign *is* salvation; even as our beloved brother Paul also according to the wisdom given unto him has written unto you;

2Pe. 3:16 As also in all *his* epistles, **speaking in them of these things; in which are some things hard to be understood, which they that are unlearned and unstable wrest, as *they do* also the other scriptures unto their own destruction**.

2Pe. 3:17 You therefore, beloved, seeing you know *these things* before, beware lest you also, being led away with the err for the wicked, fall from your own steadfastness.

2Pe. 3:18 But grow in favor, and *in* the knowledge of our Sovereign and Savior Yahusha ^(replaced with Yeshua/Jesus) Messiah. To him *be* glory both now and ever. Amen.

Paul Kept the Sabbath

Acts 17:2 And Paul, as his manner was, went in unto them, and three

Sabbath days reasoned with them out of the scriptures,

Acts 13:14 But when they departed from Perga, they came to Antioch in Pisidia, and went into the synagogue on the Sabbath day, and sat down.
Acts 13:15 And after the reading of the law and the prophets the rulers of the synagogue sent unto them, saying, *You* men *and* brethren, if ye have any word of exhortation for the people, say on.

Acts 13:42 And when the Jews were gone out of the synagogue, the Gentiles besought that these words might be preached to them the next Sabbath.
Acts 13:43 Now when the congregation was broken up, many of the Jews and religious proselytes followed Paul and Barnabas: who, speaking to them, persuaded them to continue in the favor of Elohim
(Mighty one(s)/God)
.

Acts 13:44 And the next Sabbath day came almost the whole city together to hear the word of Elohim ^{(Mighty one(s)/God)}.
Acts 13:45 But when the Jews saw the multitudes, they were filled with envy, and spoke against those things that were spoken by Paul, contradicting and blaspheming.
Acts 15:21 For Moses of old time has in every city them that preach him, being read in the synagogues every Sabbath day.

HEBREWS

Hebrews Clement of Alexandria says, that Paul wrote to the Hebrews, and that this was the opinion of Pantaenus, who was at the head of the celebrated believers school at Alexandria, and who flourished about 180 A.D. Pantaenus lived near Palestine. He must have been acquainted with the prevailing opinions on the subject, and his witness must be regarded as proof that the Epistle was regarded as Paul's by the church in that region. Origen, also of Alexandria, ascribes the Epistle to Paul; though he says that the "sentiments" are those of Paul, but that the words and phrases belong to some one relating the apostle's sentiments, and as it were commenting on the words of his leader. The witness of the church at Alexandria was uniform after the time of Origen, that it was the production of Paul. Indeed there seems never to have been any doubt in regard to it there, and from the commencement it was admitted as his production. The arguments in support of the opinion that it was written in Hebrew are, briefly, the following:(1) The witness of the fathers. Thus, Clement of Alexandria says, "Paul wrote to the Hebrews in the Hebrew language, and Luke carefully translated it into Greek." Jerome says, "Paul as a Hebrew wrote to the Hebrews in Hebrew - Scripserat ut Hebraeus Hebraeis Hebraice;" and then he adds, "this Epistle was translated into Greek, so that the coloring of the style was made diverse in this way from that of Paul's."

CHAPTER 7

Heb. 7:11 Truly, then, if perfection was through the Levitical priestly office (for the people had been given Law under it), why yet *was there* need *for* another priest to arise according to the order of Melchizedek and not to be called according to the order of Aaron?

John Gill's commentary
For under it the people received the law: not the "moral" law, which was given to Adam in innocence, and as it came by Moses, it was before the Levitical priesthood took place; but the ceremonial law, and which was carnal, mutable, and made nothing perfect: the Syriac version renders it, "by which a law was imposed upon the people"; to regard the office of priesthood, and the priests in it, and bring their sacrifices to them; and the Arabic version reads, "the law of a the priest's office"; which office was after the law of a carnal commandment, and so imperfect, as is manifest from what follows: for had perfection been by it, **Heb. 10:1** For the Law had a shadow of the coming good things, not the image *itself* of *those* things. *Appearing* year by year with the same sacrifices, which they offer continually, they never are able to perfect the ones drawing near.
Heb. 10:2 Otherwise, would they not have ceased to be offered? Because those serving did not still have conscience of sins, having once been cleansed.

Col. 2:10 and having been filled [complete], you are in Him, who is the Head of all rule and authority,
Heb. 7:12 For the priestly office having been changed [G3346], of necessity a change [G3331] of law also occurs.

- G3346 metatithemi, transfer, transport, exchange
- G3331 metathesis, transportation, change, translation.

Heb. 7:18 For, indeed, an annulment of *the* preceding command comes about because of its weakness and un-profitableness.
Acts 13:39 And everyone believing in this One is justified from all things which you could not be justified by the Law of Moses.

Rom. 8:3 For the Law *being* powerless, in that it was weak through the flesh, Elohim ^{(Mighty one(s)/God)} sending His own Son in *the* likeness of sinful flesh, and concerning sin, condemned sin in the flesh,
Rom. 8:4 so that the righteous demand of the Law might be fulfilled in us, those not walking according to flesh, but according to Spirit.

The Son was sent in the likeness of sinful flesh to condemn sin not the law, but sin in the flesh so that the law could be fulfilled in us. So we are free to walk in the spirit and not in sin.

CHAPTER 8

Heb. 8:6 But now He has gotten a more excellent ministry, also by so much as He is a Mediator of a better covenant, which has been enacted ^(G3549) on better promises.

G3549 nomotheteo-establish, receive law (Heb 7:11)
Νενομοθηται [Strong's G3549], "was ordained (or established) by law."
Receiving of the Law upon better promises Jeremiah 31:31<--new covenant...the Law on the heart, forgiveness of sins

Heb 9:15 And because of this He is Mediator of a new covenant, so that death having occurred for redemption of transgressions under the first covenant, those being called might receive the promise of the everlasting inheritance.

Heb. 12:24 and to Yahusha ^(replaced with Yeshua/Jesus) the Mediator of a new covenant, and to blood of sprinkling speaking better things than *that* of Abel.

Heb. 8:7 For if that first *covenant* had been faultless, then should no place have been sought for the second.

Heb. 8:8 For finding fault, He said to them, "Behold, days are coming, says Yahuah ^(Replaced with Lord/God), and I will make an end on the house of Israel and on the house of Judah; a new covenant *shall be*,

Heb 8:9 not according to the covenant which I made with their fathers in *the* day of My taking hold of their hand to lead them out of the land of Egypt; because they did not continue in My covenant, and I did not regard them, says Yahuah ^(Replaced with Lord/God).

Heb. 8:10 Because this *is* the covenant which I will covenant with the house of Israel after those days, says Yahuah ^(Replaced with Lord/God), giving My Laws into their mind, and I will write them on their hearts, and I will be their Elohim ^{(Mighty one(s)/God)}, and they shall be My people."

Heb. 8:11 "And they shall no more teach each one their neighbor, and each one his brother, saying, Know Yahuah ^(Replaced with Lord/God); because all shall know Me, from the least of them to their great ones.

Heb. 8:12 For I will be merciful to their un-righteousness, and I will not at all remember their sins and their lawless deeds." *LXX-Jer. 38:31-34; MT -Jer. 31:31-34*

Heb 8:13 In the saying, New, He has made the first old. And the thing being made old and growing aged *is* near disappearing.

Jdg. 2:1 And the angel of Yahuah ^(Replaced with Lord/God) came up from Gilgal to The Place of weeping, & said, I caused you to come up out of Egypt and brought you into the land which I had sworn to your fathers, & said, I will not break My covenant with you forever.

Hos. 3:4 For the sons of Israel shall remain many days *with* no king and no ruler, and with no sacrifice, and no pillars, and no ephod or teraphim.

Hos. 3:5 Afterward the sons of Israel shall return and seek Yahuah ^(Replaced with Lord/God) their Elohim ^{(Mighty one(s)/God)} and David their king. And they shall fear Yahuah ^(Replaced with Lord/God) and His goodness in the ends of the days.

Jer. 33:20 So says Yahuah ^(Replaced with Lord/God), If you can break My covenant of the day, and My covenant of the night and there should not be day and night in their time,

Jer. 33:21 *then* My covenant with My servant David may also be broken, that he should not have a son to reign on his throne, and with the Levitical priests, My ministers.

Jer. 33:22 As the host of the heavens cannot be numbered, nor the sand of the sea measured, so I will multiply the seed of My servant David, and the Levites who minister to Me.

Jer. 33:23 And the Word of Yahuah ^(Replaced with Lord/God) was to Jeremiah, saying,

Jer. 33:24 Have you not observed what these people have spoken, saying, The two families that Yahuah ^(Replaced with Lord/God) has chosen, He has also rejected them? And they despise My people, no more to be a nation before them.

Jer. 33:25 So says Yahuah ^(Replaced with Lord/God), If My covenant *is* not with day and night, *and if* I have not appointed the ordinances of the heavens and earth,

Jer. 33:26 then I also will reject the seed of Jacob, and My servant David, not to take of his seed *to be* rulers over the seed of Abraham, Isaac and Jacob. For I will bring back their captivity and have pity on them.

Ezek. 44:10 But the Levites who have gone far from Me, when Israel went astray, who went astray from Me, *going* after their idols, even they shall bear their iniquity.

Ezek. 44:11 Yet they shall be ministers in My sanctuary, overseers at the gates of the house, and ministering in the house. They shall slaughter the burnt offering and the sacrifice for the people, and they shall stand before them, to minister to them.

Ezek. 44:12 Because they ministered to them before their idols, and became a stumbling block of iniquity to the house of Israel, therefore I have lifted up My hand against them, declares Sovereign Yahuah ^(Replaced with Lord/God). And they shall bear their iniquity.

Ezek. 44:13 And they shall not come near to Me to serve as priest to Me, nor come near to any of My Holy things, to the most Holy of the Holy things, but they shall bear their shame and their abominations which they have done.

Ezek. 44:14 But I will give them *to be* keepers of the charge of the house for all its service, and for all that shall be done in it.

Ezek. 44:15 But the priests, the Levites, the sons of Zadok, who kept the charge of My sanctuary when the sons of Israel went astray from Me, they shall come near to Me to minister to Me. And they shall

stand before Me to bring near to
Me the fat and the blood, declares Sovereign Yahuah (Replaced with Lord/God).

Ezek. 44:16 They shall enter into My sanctuary, and they shall come near to My table, to minister to Me. And they shall keep My charge.
Ezek. 44:17 And it shall be when they enter in the gates of the inner court, they shall be clothed with bleached *linen* garments. And wool shall not come upon them while they minister in the gates of the inner court, and in the house.

Rev. 1:6 and made us kings and priests to Elohim (Mighty one(s)/God), even His Father. To Him *is* the glory and the might forever and ever Amen.

Rev. 5:9 And they sing a new song, saying, Worthy are You to receive the scroll, and to open its seals, because You were slain, and by Your blood purchased us to Elohim (Mighty one(s)/God) out of every tribe and tongue and people and nation,
Rev. 5:10 and made us kings and priests to our Elohim (Mighty one(s)/God), and we shall reign over the earth.

Ezek. 16:60 But I will remember My covenant with you in the days of your youth, and I will raise up to you an everlasting covenant.
Ezek. 16:61 Then you shall remember your ways and be ashamed, when you shall receive your sisters, the older than you to the younger than you, and I will give them to you for daughters, but not by your covenant.
Ezek. 16:62 And, I *even*, I will raise up My covenant with you. And you shall know that I *am* Yahuah (Replaced with Lord/God),
Ezek. 16:63 so that you may remember and be ashamed. And *you* will not any more open *your* mouth, because of your humiliation, when I am propitiated for you for all that you have done, declares Sovereign Yahuah (Replaced with Lord/God).

Isa. 66:19 And I will set a sign among them, and I will send those who escape from them to the nations of Tarshish, Pul, and Lud, drawers of the bow; *to* Tubal and Javan, *to* the far away coasts that have not heard My fame nor seen My glory. And they shall declare My glory among the nations.
Isa. 66:20 And they shall bring all your brothers out of all nations, an

offering to Yahuah ^(Replaced with Lord/God), on horses, and in chariots, and in litters, and on mules, and on camels, to My Holy mountain Jerusalem, says Yahuah ^(Replaced with Lord/God); as the sons of Israel bring the offering in a clean vessel *to* the house of Yahuah ^(Replaced with Lord/God). Isa. 66:21 And I will also take some of them for the priests, for the Levites, says Yahuah ^(Replaced with Lord/God).

Ex. 40:15 And you shall anoint them as you anointed their father. And they shall serve as priests to Me. And their anointing shall be for an everlasting priesthood for their generations.

Num. 25:11 Phinehas the son of Eleazar, the son of Aaron the priest, has turned My wrath away from the sons of Israel while he was zealous for My sake among them, so that I did not consume the sons of Israel in My jealousy.
Num. 25:12 Therefore say, Behold, I give to him My covenant of peace.
Num. 25:13 And it shall be to him, and to his seed after him, the covenant of an everlasting priesthood, because he was zealous for his Elohim ^{(Mighty one(s)/God)}, and atoned for the sons of Israel.

Isa. 66:20 And they shall bring all your brothers out of all nations, an offering to Yahuah ^(Replaced with Lord/God), on horses, and in chariots, and in litters, and on mules, and on camels, to My Holy mountain Jerusalem, says Yahuah ^(Replaced with Lord/God); as the sons of Israel bring the offering in a clean vessel *to* the house of Yahuah ^(Replaced with Lord/God). Isa. 66:21 And I will also take some of them for the priests, for the Levites, says Yahuah ^(Replaced with Lord/God). See *Hebrews 8:13*

COVENANT FOREVER

Jdg. 2:1 And an angel of Yahuah ^(Replaced with Lord/God) came up from Gilgal to Bochim, and said, I made you to go up out of Egypt, and have brought you unto the land, which I swore unto your fathers; and I said, **I will never break my covenant with you**.

Sir. 17:11 Beside this he gave them knowledge, and the law of life for an heritage.
Sir. 17:12 He made an everlasting covenant with them, and showed

them his judgments.

Ezek. 16:59 For thus says Yahuah ^(Replaced with Lord/God) Elohim ^{(Mighty one(s)/God)}; I will even deal with you as you have done, which have **despised the oath in breaking the covenant.**
Ezek. 16:60 Nevertheless I will remember my covenant with you in the days of your youth, and I will establish unto you an everlasting covenant.

The Greek seems to indicate that the Sinai covenant is old and dying off, but a closer examination of the Aramaic & Hebrew gives the picture of the Sinai covenant being broken by Israel and not able to bring the forgiveness of the Old covenant so the ^{re}New covenant is added or the old covenant is renewed or made anew. Verse 13 speaks about the new causing the old to wax old and decay.

Lamsa(Aramaic)

Heb 9:2 For the first tabernacle that was made, had in it the candlestick, and the table and the showbread; and it was called the sanctuary.
Heb 9:3 But the inner tabernacle, which is within the veil of the second door, was called the Holy of most Holy.
Heb 9:6 The priests always entered into the outer tabernacle and performed their service of worship;
Heb 9:7 But into the inner tabernacle, the high priest entered alone, once every year, with the blood which he offered for himself, and for the faults of the people.

CHAPTER 10

Did Paul teach against the Law? Points needed to understand as we keep studying the letters of Paul (PAUL ANTI-LAW)

1. Paul learned from Gamaliel (Acts 5:34) and was a brilliant scholar (Acts 22:3).
2. He was a Pharisee. Philippians 3:5-6; Acts 26:5

3. Paul taught that the Law is sound teaching. 1 Timothy 1:8-11

- **1Tim. 1:8** But we know that the law *is* good, if a man use it lawfully;
  1Tim. 1:9 Knowing this, that the law is not made for a righteous man, but for the lawless and disobedient, for the ungodly and for sinners, for unholy and profane, for murderers of fathers and murderers of mothers, for manslayers,
  1Tim. 1:10 For whoremongers, for them that defile themselves with mankind, for slave trader, for liars, for perjured persons, and if there be any other thing that is contrary to sound doctrine;
  1Tim. 1:11 According to the esteemed good news of the blessed Elohim ^{(Mighty one(s)/God)}, which was committed to my trust

4. Taught that the words of Yahusha ^(replaced with Yeshua/Jesus) are Primary.

- **1Ti. 6:3** If any man teach otherwise, and consent not to **wholesome** ^(UNCORRUPT/TRUE) **words**, *even* the **words of our Sovereign Yahusha** ^(replaced with Yeshua/Jesus) **Messiah**, and to the doctrine which is according to righteousness;
  1Ti. 6:4 He is **proud, knowing nothing**, but **doting about questions and strife's of words**, whereof comes envy, strife, railings, evil surmising,
  1Ti. 6:5 Perverse disputing of men of corrupt minds, and **destitute of the truth**, supposing that gain is righteousness: from such withdraw yourself.

5. The Old Testament is Wisdom 2 Timothy 3:15-16
6. Believed all things in the Old Testament Acts 24:14
7. The Words of the prophet's and law is scripture. Romans 16:26 & 1 Corinthians 14:21
8. He obeyed the Law. Acts 25:8
9. He taught the Law **Rom 15:18**
10. He taught the Law is good. Romans 3:31; 7:12
11. He observed the Sabbath Acts 13:42; 17:2; 18:4
12. He followed the Messiah 1 Corinthians 11:1

Did Paul teach against the Law? And if he did, should we regard his writings as scripture?

POINT #1. Yahusha ^(replaced with Yeshua/Jesus) is the "Testator of the new or ^{re}newed Covenant ^(Testament) If the Law is done away only He could have done away with it *Heb. 9:15-17.* Yahusha ^(replaced with Yeshua/Jesus) did not come to destroy the Law.

- Matt. 5:17 Think not that I am come to destroy the law, or the prophets: I am not come to destroy, but to fulfill.

- Isa. 42:21 Yahuah ^(Replaced with Lord/God) is well pleased for his righteousness' sake; **he will magnify the law**, and make *it* honorable.

  Paul's teachings must agree with the Messiah and the Scriptures.

POINT #2. The definition of a false prophet is one that turns the people away from the Law.

- **Deut. 13:1** If there arise among you a prophet, or a dreamer of dreams, and gives you a sign or a wonder,

  Deut. 13:2 And the sign or the wonder come to pass, whereof he spoke unto you, saying, Let us go after other mighty ones, which you have not known, and let us serve them;

  Deut. 13:3 You shall not hearken unto the words of that prophet, or that dreamer of dreams: for Yahuah ^(Replaced with Lord/God) your Elohim ^{(Mighty one(s)/God)} prove you, to know whether you love Yahuah ^(Replaced with Lord/God) your Elohim ^{(Mighty one(s)/God)} with all your heart and with all your soul.

  Deut. 13:4 **You shall walk after Yahuah ^(Replaced with Lord/God) your Elohim ^{(Mighty one(s)/God)}, and fear him, and keep his commandments, and obey his voice, and you shall serve him, and cleave unto him.**

POINT #3 The Scriptures defines a false witness as one who teaches that the Law is done away with.

- **Acts 6:12** And they stirred up the people, and the elders, and the scribes, and came upon *him*, and caught him, and brought *him* to the council,

  Acts 6:13 And set up **false witnesses**, which said, This man ceases not to speak blasphemous words against this Holy place, **and the Law**:

Acts 6:14 For **we have heard him say, that this Yahusha** [replaced with Yeshua/Jesus] **of Nazareth** shall destroy this place, & **shall change the customs, which Moses delivered us**.

POINT #4. In the 1st century there were rumors that Paul taught the Law was done away

- **Acts 21:20** And when they heard *it*, they esteemed Yahuah [Replaced with Lord/God], and said unto him, You see, brother, how many thousands of Jews there are which believe; and they are all **zealous of the law**:

  Acts 21:21 And **they are informed of you, that you teach** all the Jews which are among the Gentiles **to forsake Moses**, saying that they ought not to circumcise *their* children, neither to walk after the customs.

  Acts 21:22 What is it therefore? the multitude must needs come together: for they will hear that you are come.

  Acts 21:23 Do therefore this that we say to you: We have four men, which have a vow on them;

  Acts 21:24 Them take, and purify yourself with them, and be at charges with them, that they may shave *their* heads: **and all may know that those things, whereof they were informed concerning you, are nothing; but *that* you yourself also walk orderly, and keep the Law.**

  Acts 21:26 **Then Paul took the men, and the next day purifying himself with them entered into the temple**, to signify the accomplishment of the days of purification, until that an offering should be offered for every one of them.

Peter also warned about these false rumors

- **2Pe. 3:15** And account *that* the longsuffering of our Sovereign *is* salvation; even as our **beloved brother Paul** also according to the wisdom given unto him has written unto you;

  2Pe. 3:16 **As also in all** *his* **epistles, speaking in them of these things; in which are some things hard to be understood,** which **they that are unlearned and unstable wrest, as** *they do* **also the other scriptures, unto their own destruction.**

2Pe. 3:17 You therefore, beloved, seeing you know *these things* before, **beware lest you also**, **being led away** with **the error of the wicked** [(LAWLESS)], fall from your own steadfastness.

PHILIPPIANS

CHAPTER 1

Php. 1:15 Some, indeed, even proclaim Messiah because of envy and strife, but some also because of good will. [Two types].
Php. 1:16 These, indeed, announce Messiah out of party spirit, not sincerely, thinking to add affliction to my bonds.
Php. 1:17 But these *others* out of love, knowing that I am set for defense of the good news.
Php. 1:18 What then? Yet in every way, whether in pretense or in truth, Messiah is proclaimed, and I rejoice in this; yet also I will rejoice. Believers, but not followers

Mar. 9:38 And John answered Him, saying, Teacher, we saw someone casting out demons in Your name, who does not follow us. And we forbade him, because he does not follow us.
Mar. 9:39 But Yahusha [(replaced with Yeshua/Jesus)] said, Do not forbid him. For there is no one who shall do a work of power in My name, yet be able to speak evil of Me quickly.
Mar. 9:40 For who is not against us is for us.

CHAPTER 2

Php. 2:12 So, then, my beloved, even as you always **obeyed**, not as in my presence only, but now much rather in my absence, cultivate your salvation with fear and trembling,
Php. 2:13 for it is Elohim [(Mighty one(s)/God)] who is working in you both to will and to work for the sake of *His* good pleasure.

- 1Jn 4:4 Little children, you are of Elohim [(Mighty one(s)/God)] and have overcome them, because He in you is greater than he in the world.

109

Php. 2:14 Do all things without murmurings and disputing,

Php. 2:15 that you may be blameless and harmless, children of Elohim ^{(Mighty one(s)/God)}, without fault in the midst of a crooked generation, even having been perverted, among whom you shine as luminaries in *the* world,

Php. 2:16 holding up *the* Word of Life, for a boast to me in *the* day of Messiah, that I ran not in vain, nor labored in vain.

Deut. 32:4 *He is* the Rock; His work *is* perfect. For all His ways *are* just, a Elohim ^{(Mighty one(s)/God)} of faithfulness, and without evil; just and upright *is* He.

Deut. 32:5 They have corrupted themselves; *they are* not His sons; *it is* their blemish; *they are* a crooked and perverse generation.

1Joh. 1:1 What was from the beginning, what we have heard, what we have seen with our eyes, what we beheld, and *what* our hands touched, as regards the Word of Life.

Php. 1:11 being filled *with* fruits of righteousness through Yahusha ^(replaced with Yeshua/Jesus) Messiah, to *the* glory and praise of Elohim ^{(Mighty one(s)/God)}.

Yahuah ^(Replaced with Lord/God) is a light to us

- **2Sa. 22:29** For you are my lamp, O SOVEREIGN: and Yahuah ^(Replaced with Lord/God) will lighten my darkness

- **Mic. 7:8** Rejoice not against me, O mine enemy: when I fall, I shall arise; when I sit in darkness, Yahuah ^(Replaced with Lord/God) *shall be* a light unto me.

- **Psa. 27:1** Yahuah ^(Replaced with Lord/God) *is* my light and my salvation; whom shall I fear? Yahuah ^(Replaced with Lord/God) *is* the strength of my life; of whom shall I be afraid?

- **Isa. 60:19** The sun shall be no more your light by day; neither for brightness shall the moon give light unto you: but Yahuah ^(Replaced with Lord/God) shall be unto you an everlasting light, and your Elohim ^{(Mighty one(s)/God)} your glory.

110

- **Rev. 22:5** And there shall be no night there and they need no candle, neither light of the sun for Yahuah ^(Replaced with Lord/God) Elohim ^{(Mighty one(s)/God)} gives them light and they shall reign forever & ever.

The Messiah is the Light

- **Joh. 1:9** *That* was the true Light, which lights every man that come into the world.

- **Joh. 8:12** Then spoke Yahusha ^(replaced with Yeshua/Jesus) again unto them, saying, I am the light of the world: he that follows me shall not walk in darkness, but shall have the light of life.

- **Joh. 9:5** As long as I am in the world, I am the light of the world. *Isa 9:2* The people that walked in darkness have seen a great light: they that dwell in the land of the shadow of death, upon them have the light shined.

The Word is Light

- **Psa. 119:105**. Your word *is* a lamp unto my feet, and a light unto my path.

The Law is light

- **Pro. 6:23** For the commandment *is* a lamp; and the law *is* light; and reproofs of instruction *are* the way of life:

We are to be lights in the world, reflecting His light:

- **Matt. 5:14 You are the light of the world**. A city that is set on a hill cannot be hid.
  Matt. 5:15 Neither do men light a candle, and put it under a bushel, but on a candlestick; and it gives light unto all that are in the house.
  Matt. 5:16 Let your light so shine before men, that they may

see your good works, and glory your Father which is in heaven.

Phi. 2:12 Wherefore, my beloved, as you have always obeyed, not as in my presence only, but now much more in my absence, work out your own salvation with fear and trembling.

Phi. 2:13 For it is Elohim [Mighty one(s)/God] that work in you both to will and to do good of His pleasure.

Phi. 2:14 Do all things without murmurings and disputing:

Phi. 2:15 That you may be blameless and harmless, the sons of Elohim [Mighty one(s)/God], without rebuke, in the midst of a crooked and perverse nation, among whom you shine as lights in the world;

- 2Co. 4:3 But if our good news be hid, it is hid to them that are lost:

  2Co. 4:4 In whom the Elohim [Mighty one(s)/God] of this world has blinded the minds of them that believe not, lest the light of the esteemed good news of Messiah, who is the image of Elohim [Mighty one(s)/God], should shine unto them.

  2Co. 4:5 For we preach not ourselves, but Messiah Yahusha [replaced with Yeshua/Jesus] Sovereign; and ourselves your servants for Yahusha's [replaced with Yeshua/Jesus] sake.

  2Co. 4:6 For Elohim [Mighty one(s)/God], who commanded the light to shine out of darkness, have shined in our hearts, to *give* the light of the knowledge of the glory of Elohim [Mighty one(s)/God] in the face of Yahusha [replaced with Yeshua/Jesus] Messiah.

- *Luk. 12:31-35* But rather **seek you the kingdom of Elohim** [Mighty one(s)/God]; and all these things shall be added unto you.

  Luk. 12:32 Fear not, little flock; for it is your Father's good pleasure to give you the kingdom.

  Luk. 12:33 Sell that you have, and give alms; provide yourselves bags which wax not old, a treasure in the heavens that fail not, where no thief approach, neither moth corrupt.

  Luk. 12:34 For where your treasure is, there will your heart be also.

  Luk. 12:35 Let your loins be girded about [*Eph 6:14*] Stand therefore, having your **loins girt about with truth**, and having on the breastplate of righteousness; and *your* **lights burning**

Look at the pattern. The Father is light, The Son is light. The Word is light, the Law is light. (All four are light and) Having the Father and the Son, His Word and His Law will make us a light. This is how we become a light to the World.

The Law and the Word of Yahuah ^(Replaced with Lord/God) will go forth out of Zion

- **Isa. 2:3** And many people shall go and say, Come ye, and let us
go up to the mountain of Yahuah ^(Replaced with Lord/God), to the house of the Elohim ^{(Mighty one(s)/God)} of Jacob; and he will teach us of his ways, and we will walk in his paths: **for out of Zion shall go forth the law, and the word of Yahuah** ^(Replaced with Lord/God) **from Jerusalem**.

Zion is a people

- **Isa. 51:15** But I *am* Yahuah ^(Replaced with Lord/God) your Elohim ^{(Mighty one(s)/God)}, which divided the sea, whose waves roared: Yahuah ^(Replaced with Lord/God) of hosts *is* his name.
Isa. 51:16 And I have put my words in your mouth, and I have covered you in the shadow of mine hand, that I may plant the heavens, and lay the foundations of the earth, and **say unto Zion, You** *are* **my people**.

Matt. 21:5 Tell the daughter of Zion, behold, your King is coming unto you, meek, and sitting upon an ass, and a colt the foal of an ass. [See. Is. 2:3].

Rom. 11:26 And so all Israel shall be saved: as it is written, there shall come out of Zion the Deliverer, and shall turn away the ungodliness from Jacob;

Rev. 14:1 And I looked, and, lo, a Lamb stood on the mount Zion, and with Him an hundred forty and four thousand, having His Father's name written in their foreheads.

The daughter of Zion are Israel His people and those that want to be apart of Israel can *Eph. 2:10-12*

We are the branches of the menorah

- **Joh. 15:1** I am the true vine, and my Father is the husbandman. Joh. 15:5 I am the vine, you *are* **the branches**
  - ○ {**G2814** κληη μα klema a *limb* or *shoot* (as **if broken off):** - branch.}: He that abides in me, and I in him, the same brings forth much fruit: for without me you can do nothing.
- The branches must do what the vine does, or produces. He was not lawless neither should we be lawless. We walk just how He walked. Being obedient to the Fathers word.

Branches = Netsariym

- **Acts 24:5** For we have found this man *a* pestilent *fellow*, and a mover of sedition among all the Jews throughout the world, and a ringleader of the **sect of the Nazarenes:**

- **Jer. 31:6** For there shall be a day, *that* **the watchmen**
  - ○ {**H5341** נצר natsar נצרים} upon the mount Ephraim shall cry, Arise you, and let us go up to Zion unto Yahuah ^(Replaced with Lord/God) our Elohim ^{(Mighty one(s)/God)}.

Isa. 11:1 And there shall come forth a rod out of the stem of Jesse, and a **Branch**{**H5342** נצר netser} shall grow out of his roots:

Isa. 60:21 Your people also *shall be* all righteous: they shall inherit the land forever, the branch{**H5342** netser} of my planting, the work of my hands, that I may be esteemed.

Isa. 49:6 And he said, It is a light thing that you should be my servant to raise up the tribes of Jacob, and to restore the preserved {**H5341 natsar**} of Israel: I will also give you for a light to the Gentiles, that you may be my salvation unto the end of the earth.

114

- <u>Luke 1:32</u> He shall be great, and shall be called the Son of the Highest: and the Sovereign Elohim ^{(Mighty one(s)/God)} shall give unto him the throne of his father David:
- <u>Luke 1:33</u> And he shall reign over the house of Jacob forever; and of his kingdom there shall be no end

Matt. 2:23 And he came and dwelt in a city called Nazareth: that it might be fulfilled which was spoken by the prophets, **He shall be called a Nazarene.**

- ß-Isa. 11:1...Nazarene = Netser/Netserim/Natsarim/Branches *His disciples have the witness of Messiah* ^(Light) *and keep His commandments/Law* ^(Light)

- **Isa. 8:16 Bind up the witness, seal the law among my disciples**.

- **Isa. 8:20** To the law and to the witness: if they speak not according to this word, *it is* because *there is* no light in them.

- **Rev. 12:17** And the dragon was wroth with the woman, and went to make
war with the remnant of her seed, **which keep the commandments of
Elohim** ^{(Mighty one(s)/God)}**, and have the witness of Yahusha** <sup>(replaced with
Yeshua/Jesus)</sup> **Messiah**.

- **Rev. 14:12** Here is the patience of the saints are they that keep the commandments of Elohim ^{(Mighty one(s)/God)}, and the faith of Yahusha ^(replaced with Yeshua/Jesus).

CHAPTER 3

Was Paul telling the Philippians to beware of circumcision or of the circumcision party? Even though a person is circumcised, he would not be considered circumcised to a Pharisee unless he was circumcised according to the rites of the oral law
    1) Hatafat Dan Brit – Drawing of Blood.
    2) Periah – Pulling Back of The Corona.

3) Metsitsah – Sucking Blood.

Perhaps this is what Paul is speaking of in his letter to the Philippians

Php. 3:2 Look out *for* the dogs, look out *for* the evil workers, look out *for* the concision** *party*.
Php. 3:3 For we are the circumcision, the ones who worship by the Spirit of Elohim ^{(Mighty one(s)/God)}, and who glory in Messiah Yahusha ^(replaced with Yeshua/Jesus), and who do not trust in flesh.
**

- **The concision** (*ten katatomen*). Late word for incision, mutilation (in contrast with *peritome*, circumcision). In Symmachus and an inscription. The verb *katatemno* is used in the LXX only of mutilations *(Leviticus 21:5; 1 Kings 18:28)*. Mutilation is also the word used in the Aramaic

Php. 3:4 Even though I *might* have trust in flesh; if any other thinks to trust in flesh, I more;
Php. 3:5 in circumcision, *the* eighth day, of *the* race of Israel, *the* tribe of Benjamin, a Hebrew of the Hebrews; according to Law, a Pharisee;
Php .3:6 according to zeal, persecuting the assembly; according to righteousness in Law, being blameless.
Php. 3:7 But what things was gain to me, these I have counted loss because of Messiah.
Php. 3:8 But, no, rather I also count all things to be loss because of the excellence of the knowledge of Messiah Yahusha ^(replaced with Yeshua/Jesus) my Sovereign, for whose sake I have suffered the loss of all things and count *them to be* trash, that I might gain Messiah
Php. 3:9 and be found in Him; **not having my own righteousness of Law**, but through the faith of Messiah, *having* the righteousness of Elohim ^{(Mighty one(s)/God)} on faith,
Php. 3:10 to know Him and the power of His resurrection, and the fellowship of His sufferings, having been conformed to His death,
Php. 3:11 if somehow I may attain to a resurrection out of the dead.

All things loss

Matt. 16:24 Then Yahusha ^(replaced with Yeshua/Jesus) said to His disciples, If anyone desires to come after Me, let him deny himself, and let him bear his cross, and let him follow Me.

Matt. 16:25 For whoever may desire to save his life will lose it. But whoever may lose his life for My sake will find it.

Matt. 16:26 For what will a man be benefited if he should gain the whole world, but forfeits his soul? Or what will a man give *as* an exchange *for* his soul?

Matt. 16:27 For the Son of Man is about to come with His angels in the glory of His Father. And then "He will give reward to each according to his practice." *LXX-Psa. 61:13; Pro. 24:12; MT-Psa. 62:12*

ROMANS

Treasury of Scripture Knowledge Commentary

..The whole Epistle is to be taken in connection, or considered as one continued discourse; and the sense of every part must be taken from the drift of the whole. Every sentence, or verse, is not to be regarded as a distinct mathematical proposition, or theorem, or as a sentence in the book of Proverbs, whose sense is absolute, and

independent of what goes before, or comes after, but we must remember, that every sentence, especially in the argumentative part, bears relation to, and is dependent upon, the whole discourse, and cannot be rightly understood unless we understand the scope and drift of the whole; and therefore, the whole Epistle, or at least the eleven first chapters of it, ought to be read over at once, without stopping. As to the use and excellence of this Epistle, I shall leave it to speak for itself, when the reader has studied and well digested its contents....This Epistle will not be difficult to understand, if our minds are unprejudiced, and at liberty to attend to the subject,

and to the current scriptural sense of the words used.

Albert Barnes Introductory commentary

This Epistle has been usually deemed the most difficult of interpretation of any part of the New Testament; and no small part of the controversies in the Christian church have grown out of discussions about its meaning. Early in the history of the church, even before the death of the apostles, we learn from 2Pe. 3:16, that the writings of Paul were some of them regarded as being "hard to be understood"; and that "the unlearned and unstable wrested them to their own destruction." It is probable that Peter has reference here to the high and mysterious doctrines about justification and the sovereignty of Elohim ^{(Mighty one(s)/God)}, and the doctrines of election and decrees.

From the Epistle of James, it would seem probable also, that already the apostle Paul's doctrine of justification by faith had been perverted and abused. It seems to have been inferred that good works were unnecessary; and here was the beginning of the cheerless and withering system of Antinomianism - than which a more destructive or pestilential heresy never found its way into the Christian church.

Several reasons might be assigned for the controversies, *which* have grown out of this Epistle:

(1) The very structure of the argument, and the uniqueness of the apostle's manner of writing. Paul is rapid, mighty, profound, often involved, readily following a new thought, leaving the regular subject, and returning again after a considerable interval. Hence, his writings abound with parentheses and with complicated paragraphs.

(2) Objections are often introduced, so that it requires close attention to determine their precise bearing. Though Paul employs no small part of the Epistle in answering objections, yet an objector is never once formally introduced or mentioned.

(3) Many of Paul's expressions and phrases are liable to be misunderstood, and capable of perversion. Of this class are such expressions as "the righteousness of faith," "the righteousness of Elohim ^{(Mighty one(s)/God)}," etc.

(4) The doctrines themselves are high and mysterious. They are those subjects upon which the most profound minds have been in all ages exercised in vain. On them there has been, and always will be a difference of opinion. *Even with the most honest intentions that people ever have, they find it difficult or impossible to approach the investigation of them without the bias of early education or the prejudice of previous opinion.*

In this world, it is not given to human beings to fully understand these great doctrines. And it is not wonderful that the discussion of them have given rise to endless controversies: and that they who have: Reasoned high. Of Providence, foreknowledge, will, and fate; Fixed fate, free will, foreknowledge absolute, Have found no end, in wandering mazes lost.

(5) It cannot be denied that one reason why the epistles of Paul have been regarded as so difficult has been an unwillingness to admit the

truth of the plain doctrines, which he teaches. The heart is by nature opposed to them and comes to believe them with great reluctance. This feeling will account for no small part of the difficulties felt in regard to this Epistle. There is one great maxim in interpreting the Scriptures that can never

be departed from. It is, that people can never understand them aright, until they are willing to allow them to speak out their fair and proper meaning. *When people are determined not to find certain doctrines in the Scripture, nothing is more natural than that they should find difficulties in it, and complain much of its great obscurity and mystery.* I add, Perhaps, on the whole, there is no book of the messianic writings that demands more a humble, docile, and prayerful disposition in its interpretation than this Epistle. Its profound doctrines, its abstruse inquiries, and the opposition of many of those doctrines to the views of the un-renewed and un-subdued heart of man, make a spirit of docility and prayer especially necessary in its investigation. No one has ever understood the reasoning's and views of the apostle Paul except under the influence of elevated piety. No one has ever found opposition to his doctrines recede, and difficulties vanish, who did not bring the mind in an humble frame to receive all that has been revealed; and that, in a spirit of humble prayer, did not purpose to lay aside all bias and open the heart to the full influence of the elevated truths which the apostle Paul inculcates. Where there is a willingness that Elohim [Mighty one(s)/God] should reign and do all His pleasure, this Epistle to the Romans may, in its general character, be easily understood. Where this is something lacking, it will appear full of mystery and perplexity; the mind will be embarrassed, and the heart dissatisfied with its doctrines; and the un-humbled spirit will rise from its study only confused, irritated, perplexed, and dissatisfied.

Who are the Romans?

Maccabees
1Ma. 12:1 Now when Jonathan saw that time served him, he chose certain men, and sent them to Rome, for to confirm and renew the friendship that they had with them.
1Ma. 12:2 He sent letters also to the Lacedemonians, and to other places, for the same purpose.
1Ma. 12:3 So they went unto Rome, and entered into the senate, and

said, Jonathan the high priest and the people of the Jews, sent us unto you, to the end you should renew the friendship, which you had with them, and league, as in former time.

1Ma. 12:4 Upon this the Romans gave them letters unto the governors of every place that they should bring them into the land of Judea peaceably.

1Ma. 12:5 And this is the copy of the letters which Jonathan wrote to the Lacedemonians:

1Ma. 12:6 Jonathan the high priest, and the elders of the nation, and the priests, and the other of **the Jews, unto the Lacedemonians their brethren** send greeting:

1Ma. 12:7 There were letters sent in times past unto Onias the high priest from Darius, who reigned then among you, to signify that **you are our brethren**, as the copy here underwritten doth specify.

1Ma. 12:8 At which time Onias entreated the ambassador that was sent honorably, and received the letters, wherein declaration was made of the league and friendship.

1Ma. 12:9 Therefore we also, albeit we need none of these things, that we have the Holy books of scripture in our hands to comfort us,

1Ma. 12:10 Have nevertheless attempted to send unto you for the renewing of brotherhood and friendship, lest we should become strangers unto you altogether: for there is a long time passed since ye sent unto us.

1Ma. 12:11 We therefore at all times without ceasing, both in our feasts, and other convenient days, do remember you in the sacrifices which we offer, and in our prayers, as reason is, and as it becomes us to think upon our brethren:

1Ma. 12:20 Areus king of the Lacedemonians to Onias the high priest, greeting:

1Ma. 12:21 It is found in writing, that the Lacedemonians and Jews are brethren, and that they are of the stock of Abraham:

1Ma. 14:40 For he had heard say, that the Romans had called the Jews their friends and confederates and brethren; and that they had entertained the ambassadors of Simon honorably;

Who or what are Lacedemonians? They are Spartans
(Geneva) The King of the Spartians vnto Onias the high Priest sends

greeting.
(Vulgate) rex Spartiarum Onias Ionathae sacerdoti magno salutem

CHAPTER 1

Faith = Obedience

Rom. 1:5 by whom we received favor and apostleship to obedience of faith among all the nations, for His name's sake,

Who's Who?

- **Rom. 1:13** Now I would not have you ignorant, brethren, that oftentimes I purposed to come unto you, (but was let hitherto,) that I might have some fruit among you also, even as among other Gentiles.
Rom. 1:14 I am debtor both to the Greeks, and to the Barbarians; both to the wise, and to the unwise.

Why does Paul make a distinction between Greeks and Barbarians? Who are the Greeks?

The Dispersion

- **Joh. 7:35** Then the Jews said amongst themselves, Where is this One about to go that we will not find Him? Is He about to go to **the Dispersion of the Greeks**, and to teach the Greeks?
- **James** 1:1 James, a servant of Elohim ^{(Mighty one(s)/God)} and of the Sovereign Yahusha ^(replaced with Yeshua/Jesus) Messiah, to the twelve tribes which are scattered abroad, greeting.

Greek believers kept the feasts

- **Joh. 12:20** And there were some Greeks among those coming up, that they might worship at the Feast.

Greek believers met in synagogues

- **Acts 14:1** And it happened in Iconium, they went in together

121

into the synagogue of the Jews. and spoke so as for a huge multitude of both Jews and Greeks to believe.

- **Acts 18:4** And he reasoned in the synagogue on every Sabbath persuading both Jews and Greeks.

Jews and Greek believers are not to separate themselves

- **Rom. 10:12** For there is no difference both of Jew and of Greek, for the same Sovereign of all is rich toward all the ones calling on Him.

- **1Co. 10:32** Be without offense both to Jews and Greeks, and to the assembly of Elohim ^{(Mighty one(s)/God)}.

- **1Co. 12:13** For also we all were immersed by one Spirit into one body, whether Jews or Greeks, whether slaves or free, even all were given to drink into one Spirit.

- **Rom. 1:18** For Elohim(s) ^{(Mighty one(s)/God)} wrath is revealed from Heaven on all unrighteous and unrighteousness of men, holding the truth in unrighteousness,

G93 αδικια adikia
Thayer Definition:
1) injustice, of a judge
2) unrighteousness of heart and life
3) a deed violating law and justice, Acts of unrighteousness
[Unrighteousness is violation of the Law].

Rom. 2:6 Who will render to every man according to his deeds:
Rom. 2:7 To them who by patient continuance in well doing seek for glory and honor and immortality, eternal life:
Rom. 2:8 But unto them that are contentious, and do not obey the truth, **but obey unrighteousness**, indignation and wrath,

Heb. 8:12 For I will be merciful to their un-righteousness, and I will not at all remember their sins and their lawless deeds. *LXX-Jer. 38:31-34; MT -Jer. 31:31-34*

Luk. 13:27 And He will say, I tell you I do not know you, from where you are. "Stand back from Me all workers of unrighteousness! {G93 Adikia}" *Psa. 6:8*

CHAPTER 2

Rom. 2:11 For there is no respect of persons with Elohim ^{(Mighty one(s)/God)}.

Rom. 2:12 For as many as sinned without Law will also perish without Law. And as many as sinned within Law will be judged through Law. Rom. 2:13 For not the hearers of the Law are just with Elohim ^{(Mighty one(s)/God)}, but the doers of the Law shall be justified.

Luk. 12:47 But that slave knowing the will of his Sovereign, and not preparing, nor doing according to His will be beaten with many *stripes*.
Luk 12:48 But he not knowing, and doing *things* worthy of stripes, will be beaten with few. And everyone given much, much will be demanded from him. And to whom much was deposited, more exceedingly they will ask *of* him.

Matt. 7:21 Not everyone who says to Me, Sovereign, Sovereign, will enter into the kingdom of Heaven, but the *ones* who do the will of My Father in Heaven.

Heb. 5:8 though being a Son, He learned obedience from what He suffered
Heb. 5:9 and having been perfected, He came to be *the* Author of eternal salvation to all the *ones* obeying Him,
  - 1Kings 8:61 Let your heart therefore be perfect with Yahuah our Elohim ^{(Mighty one(s)/God)}, to walk in his statutes, and to keep his commandments, as at this day.

Rom. 2:14 For when nations not having Law do by nature the things of the Law, they not having Law are a law to themselves,
Rom. 2:15 who show the work of the Law written in their hearts, their conscience witnessing with *them*, and the thoughts between one another accusing or even excusing, Circumcision

Rom. 2:25 For indeed circumcision profits if you practice *the* Law, but if you are a transgressor of Law, your circumcision becomes un-circumcision.

Jer. 9:25 Behold, the days come, says Yahuah ^(Replaced with Lord/God), that I will punish all the circumcised with foreskin:
Jer. 9:26 Egypt, and Judah, and Edom, and the sons of Ammon, and Moab, and all those trimmed on the edges *of their beards, who* dwell in the wilderness. For all the nations are uncircumcised, and all the house of Israel, those uncircumcised of heart.

1Co. 7:19 Circumcision is nothing, and un-circumcision is nothing, but the keeping of Elohim(s) ^{(Mighty one(s)/God)} commands.

Why was Paul so adamant about circumcision?
Because the Jews of his time almost worshipped the Acts of circumcision more than Elohim ^{(Mighty one(s)/God)}.

"says R. Eliezar ben Azariah, un-circumcision is rejected, because by it the wicked are defiled, as it is said, "for all the Gentiles are uncircumcised"; says R. Ishmael, מילה גדולה , "great is circumcision"; for on account of it, thirteen covenants were made; says R. Jose, "great is circumcision", for it drives away the Sabbath, the weighty (command in the law,
that is, it is obliged to give way to it); R. Joshua ben Korcha says, "great is circumcision", for it was not suspended to Moses the righteous one full hour; R. Nehemiah says, "great is circumcision", for it drives away plagues; says Rabba, "great is circumcision", for notwithstanding all the commands which Abraham our father did, he was not called perfect until he was circumcised; as it is said, "walk before me, and be you perfect"; says another, "great is circumcision", for had it not been for that, the Holy blessed Elohim ^{(Mighty one(s)/God)} would not have created his world; as it is said, "thus says Yahuah ^(Replaced with Lord/God), if my covenant be not with day and night, and if I have not appointed the ordinances of heaven and earth"
"the Holy blessed Elohim ^{(Mighty one(s)/God)} (say they) rejects the uncircumcised, and brings them down to hell; as it is said, Ezek. 32:18 "son of man, wail for the multitude of Egypt, and cast them down"; and so

says Isaiah, Isa. 5:14 "therefore hell has enlarged herself and opened her mouth", חק לבלי; that is, to him that has not the law of circumcision; as it is said, Psa. 105:10 "and confirmed the same unto Jacob for a law, and to Israel for an everlasting covenant"; for no circumcised persons go down to hell:"

Rom. 2:28 For he is not a Jew that *is one* outwardly, nor *is* circumcision that outwardly in flesh;
Rom. 2:29 but he *is* a Jew that *is one* inwardly, and circumcision *is* of heart, in spirit, not in letter; of whom the praise *is* not from men, but from Elohim (Mighty one(s)/God).
What is circumcision of the heart?

Deut. 10:12 And now, Israel, what has Yahuah (Replaced with Lord/God) your Elohim (Mighty one(s)/God) asked of you, except to fear Yahuah (Replaced with Lord/God) your Elohim (Mighty one(s)/God), to walk in all His ways, and to love Him, and to serve Yahuah (Replaced with Lord/God) your Elohim (Mighty one(s)/God) with all your heart, and with all your soul;
Deut. 10:13 to keep the commandments of Yahuah (Replaced with Lord/God), and His statutes, which I am commanding you today, for your good.
Deut. 10:14 Behold, the heavens and the Heaven of the heavens, the earth and all in it, *belong* to Yahuah (Replaced with Lord/God) your Elohim (Mighty one(s)/God).
Deut. 10:15 Only, Yahuah (Replaced with Lord/God) has delighted in your father's to love them; and He chose their seed after them, on you out of all the peoples, as *it is* today.
Deut. 10:16 And you shall circumcise the foreskin of your heart and you shall not harden your neck any more.

Deut. 30:6 And Yahuah (Replaced with Lord/God) your Elohim (Mighty one(s)/God) will circumcise your heart, and the heart of your seed, to love Yahuah (Replaced with Lord/God) your Elohim (Mighty one(s)/God) with all your heart and with all your soul that you may live.
Deut. 30:7 And Yahuah (Replaced with Lord/God) your Elohim (Mighty one(s)/God) will put all these curses on your enemies, and on those that hate you, who have persecuted you.
Deut. 30:8 And you shall return and obey the voice of Yahuah (Replaced with Lord/God), and do all His commandments which I *am* commanding you today.

Lev. 26:40 And if they shall confess their iniquity, and the iniquity of their fathers, in their trespass with which they have trespassed against Me; and, also, that they have walked contrary to Me,

Lev. 26:41 *that* I also have walked contrary to them, and *I* have brought them into the land of their enemies; if their uncircumcised hearts are then humbled, and they then *have* accepted punishment for their iniquity;

Lev. 26:42 then I will remember My covenant *with* Jacob, and also My covenant with Isaac, and I shall also remember My covenant with Abraham, and I shall remember the land.

1Sa. 16:7 And Yahuah ^(Replaced with Lord/God) said to Samuel, Do not look on his appearance, nor to the height of his stature, for I have rejected him. For man does not see what He sees. For man looks for the eyes, but Yahuah ^(Replaced with Lord/God) looks for the heart.

CHAPTER 3

Rom. 3:1 What then *is* the superiority of the Jew? Or what the profit of circumcision?

Rom. 3:2 Much every way. For first indeed, that they were entrusted with the Words of Elohim ^{(Mighty one(s)/God)}.

Rom. 3:3 For what if some did not believe? shall their unbelief make the faith of Elohim ^{(Mighty one(s)/God)} without effect?

Rom. 3:4 Elohim ^{(Mighty one(s)/God)} forbid: yea, let Elohim ^{(Mighty one(s)/God)} be true, but every man a liar; as it is written, That you might be justified in your sayings, and might overcome when you are judged.

- **Psa. 51:4** Against you, you only, have I sinned, and done *this* evil in your sight that you might be justified when you speak *and* be clear when you judge.

Rom. 11:32 For Elohim ^{(Mighty one(s)/God)} shut up all into disobedience, that He may show mercy to all

Rumors

Rom. 3:8 And not (as we are wrongly accused, and as some report us to say), Let us do bad things so that good things may come, *the* judgment of whom is just .

- **Rom 6:1** What then shall we say? Shall we continue in sin that favor may abound?
- **Rom 6:15** What then? Shall we sin because we are not under Law, but under favor? Let it not be!

- **Sir. 15:20** He has commanded no man to do wickedly, neither has he given any man license to sin.

- **Acts 21:18** And on the next *day*, Paul went in with us to James. And all the elders came.

- **Acts 21:21** And they were informed about you, that you teach falling away from Moses, telling all the Jews throughout the nations not to circumcise *their* children, nor to walk in the customs.

Rom. 3:19 But we know that whatever the Law says, it speaks to those within the Law, so that every mouth may be stopped, and all the world be under judgment to Elohim ^{(Mighty one(s)/God)}.
Rom 3:20 Because by works of Law not one of all flesh will be justified before Him, for through Law *is* full knowledge of sin. *Psa. 143:2*

- **Rom. 6:14** For your sin shall not sovereign it over you, for you are not under Law, but under favor.
Rom. 6:15 What then? Shall we sin because we are not under Law, but under favor? Let it not be!
Rom. 6:16 Do you not know that to whom you present yourselves *as* slaves for obedience, you are slaves to whom you obey, whether of sin to death, or obedience to righteousness?
Rom. 6:17 But thanks *be* to Elohim ^{(Mighty one(s)/God)} that you were slaves of sin, but you obeyed from *the* heart the form of doctrine to which you were delivered.
Rom. 6:18 And having been set free from sin, you were enslaved to righteousness.

- **Gal. 5:18** But if you are led by *the* Spirit, you are not under Law.

127

- **Psa. 130:2** Sovereign, hear my voice, and let Your ears attend to the voice of my prayers.

  Psa. 130:3 If You will keep iniquities, O Yahuah ^(Replaced with Lord/God), O Sovereign, who shall stand?

  Psa. 130:4 But forgiveness *is* with You that You may be feared.

- **Psa. 143:1** *A Psalm of David.* Hear my prayer, O Yahuah ^(Replaced with Lord/God) give ear to my supplications; answer me in Your faithfulness, in Your righteousness;

  Psa. 143:2 and do not enter into judgment with Your servant; for not anyone living is just in Your sight.

- **Rom. 4:15** For the Law works out wrath; for where no law is, neither *is* transgression.

- **Rom. 7:7** What shall we say then? *Is* the Law sin? Let it not be! But I did not know sin except through Law; for also I did not know lust except the Law said, "You shall not lust." *Ex. 20:17*

  Rom. 7:8 But sin taking occasion through the commandment worked every lust in me; for apart from Law, sin *is* dead.

  Rom. 7:9 And I was alive apart from Law once, but the commandment came, and sin came alive, and I died.

  Rom. 7:10 And the commandment which *was* to life, this was found *to be* death to me;

  Rom. 7:11 for sin taking occasion through the commandment deceived me, and through it killed *me*.

  Rom. 7:12 So indeed the Law *is* Holy, and the commandment Holy and just and good.

  Rom. 7:13 Then that *which is* good, *has it* become death to me? Let it not be! But sin, that it might appear *to be* sin, having worked out death to me through the good, in order that sin might become excessively sinful through the commandment.

Rom. 3:21 But now a righteousness of Elohim ^{(Mighty one(s)/God)} has been revealed apart from Law, being witnessed by the Law and the Prophets,

- **Jer. 23:5** Behold, the days come, says Yahuah ^(Replaced with Lord/God), that I will raise to David a righteous Branch, and a King shall reign and Acts wisely, and *He* shall do justice and righteousness in the earth.
Jer. 23:6 In His days Judah shall be saved, and Israel shall dwell safely. And this is His name which He shall be called, Yahuah ^(Replaced with Lord/God) our Righteousness.

- **Dan. 9:24** Seventy weeks are decreed as to your people, and as to your Holy city, to finish the transgression, and to make an end of sin's and to make atonement for iniquity, and to bring in everlasting righteousness, and to seal up
the vision and prophecy, and to anoint the Most Holy.

- **Isa. 45:22** Turn to Me and be saved, all the ends of the earth; for I *am* Elohim ^{(Mighty one(s)/God)}, and there *is* no other.
Isa. 45:23 I have sworn by Myself, the Word has gone out of My mouth *in* righteousness, and shall not return, that to Me every knee shall bow, every tongue shall swear.
Isa. 45:24 He shall say, Only in Yahuah ^(Replaced with Lord/God) do I have righteousness and strength; to Him he comes; and they are ashamed, all who are angry with Him.

- **Isa. 51:7** Hear Me, those knowing righteousness the people of My Law in their heart do not fear the reproach of man, and do not be bowed from their blaspheming.
Isa. 51:8 For the moth shall eat them like a garment yea, the moth worm shall eat them like wool But My righteousness shall be forever, and My salvation shall be *from* generation to generation.

- **Isa. 54:17** Every weapon formed against you shall not prosper, and every tongue that shall rise against you in judgment you shall condemn. This *is* the inheritance of the servants of Yahuah ^(Replaced with Lord/God), and their righteousness *is* from Me, says Yahuah ^(Replaced with Lord/God).

- **Isa. 61:10** Rejoicing I will rejoice in Yahuah ^(Replaced with Lord/God). My soul shall be joyful in my Elohim ^{(Mighty one(s)/God)}.

For He clothed me *with* garments of salvation; He put on me the robe of righteousness, even as a bridegroom dons *himself* with ornaments, and as a bride wears her ornaments.

- **Matt. 22:11** And the king coming in to look over those reclining, he saw a man there not having been dressed *in* a wedding garment
- Matt. 22:12 And he said to him, Friend, how did you come in here, not having a wedding garment? But he was speechless. (Every mouth stopped-Romans 3:19)

Rom. 3:21 But now a righteousness of Elohim ^{(Mighty one(s)/God)} has been revealed apart from Law, being **witnessed by the Law and the Prophets**,

Rom. 3:22 even the righteousness of Elohim ^{(Mighty one(s)/God)} through faith of Yahusha ^(replaced with Yeshua/Jesus) Messiah toward all and upon all those believing; for there is no difference,

Rom. 3:23 for all sinned and fall short of the glory of Elohim ^{(Mighty one(s)/God)},

Rom. 3:24 being justified freely by His favor through the redemption in Messiah Yahusha ^(replaced with Yeshua/Jesus),

- 2 Esdras 8:35 For in truth there is no man among them that be born, but he has dealt wickedly; & among the faithful there is none which has not done amiss.
- 2 Esdras 8:36 For in this, O Sovereign, your righteousness and your goodness shall be declared, if you be merciful unto them which have not the confidence of good works.

Paul's teaching on justification and righteousness comes directly from the Law

Rom. 3:25 whom Elohim ^{(Mighty one(s)/God)} set forth *as* a propitiation through faith in His blood, as a demonstration of His righteousness through the passing over of the sins that had taken place before, in the forbearance of Elohim ^{(Mighty one(s)/God)},

Rom. 3:26 for a demonstration of His righteousness in the present time, for His being just and justifying the *one* that *is* of the faith of Yahusha ^(replaced with Yeshua/Jesus).

by FAVOR the Israelites were delivered out of Egypt

- **Ex. 3:20** And I will stretch out My hand and strike Egypt with all My wonders, which I will do in its midst, and afterward he will send you away.

  Ex. 3:21 And I will give this people **favor** in the eyes of Egypt and it will come to pass when you go, you will not go empty.

They were saved by FAITH in the BLOOD

- **Ex. 12:7** And they shall take from the blood, and put *it* on the two side doorposts and on the upper doorpost, on the houses *in* which they eat it.

  Ex 12:13 And the blood shall be to you for a token upon the houses where you are: and when I see the blood, I will pass over you, and the plague shall not be upon you to destroy you, when I smite the land of Egypt.

BOTH Israelites and Non Israelites were saved by FAITH

- **Ex. 12:37** And the sons of Israel traveled from Rameses to Succoth, the men being about six hundred thousand on foot apart from little ones.

  Ex. 12:38 And also a mixed multitude went up with them, and flocks, and herds, very many livestock.

Rom. 3:27 Then where *is* the boasting? It was excluded. Through what law? Of works? No, but through a Law of faith.

Rom. 3:28 Then we conclude a man to be justified by faith without works of Law.

- **Eph. 2:8** For by favor you are saved, through faith, and this not of yourselves; *it is* the gift of Elohim ^{(Mighty one(s)/God)};

  Eph. 2:9 not of works, that not anyone should boast;

  Eph. 2:10 for we are *His* workmanship, created in Messiah Yahusha ^(replaced with Yeshua/Jesus) unto good works, which Elohim ^{(Mighty one(s)/God)} before prepared that we should walk in them.

Rom. 3:31 Then *is* the Law annulled through faith? Let it not be! But we **establish (continue, hold up)** Law.

- Psa. 119:29 Remove from me the way of lying, and favor me

with Your Law.
Psa. 119:30 I have chosen the way of truth (emunah=faith;) I have held Your judgments level

- **Matt. 23:23** Woe to you, scribes and Pharisee's hypocrites! For you pay tithes of mint and dill and cummin, and you have left aside the weightier *matters* of the Law: judgment, and mercy, and faith. It was right to do these, and not to have left those aside. The weightier matters of the law are:
  1. Judgments
  2. Mercy
  3. FAITH

- **Rom. 7:25** I thank Elohim [(Mighty one(s)/God)] through Yahusha [(replaced with Yeshua/Jesus)] Messiah our Sovereign! So then I myself with the mind truly serve *the* Law of Elohim [(Mighty one(s)/God)], *with* the flesh *the* law of sin.

CHAPTER 4

Psa. 32:1 *A Psalm of David. A Contemplation.* Blessed *is* he whose transgression is lifted, whose sin *is* covered.
Psa. 32:2 Blessed *is* the man to whom Yahuah [(Replaced with Lord/God)] does not charge iniquity, and in whose spirit there *is* no guile.

Rom. 4:14 For if those of Law *are* heirs, faith has been made of no effect, and the promise has been annulled.
Rom. 4:15 For the Law works out wrath; for where no law is, neither *is* transgression.
  - 3709. ὀργή orge, *or-gay´;* from 3713; properly, desire (as a reaching forth or excitement of the mind), i.e. (by analogy), violent passion (ire, or (justifiable) abhorrence); by implication punishment: — anger, indignation, vengeance, wrath.

  - **2Ki. 22:13** Go, inquire of Yahuah [(Replaced with Lord/God)] for me, and for the people, and for all Judah, as to the Words of this Book that has been found; for great *is* the wrath of Yahuah [(Replaced with Lord/God)] that has been kindled against us, because our fathers have not listened to the Words of this Book, to do ac-

132

cording to all that which is written concerning us.

- **Joh. 3:36** The *one* believing into the Son has everlasting life; but the *one* disobeying the Son will not see life, but the wrath of Elohim ^{(Mighty one(s)/God)} remains on him.

- **Col. 3:4** Whenever Messiah our life is revealed, then also you will be revealed with Him in glory.
Col. 3:5 Then put to death your members which *are* on the earth: fornication, uncleanness, passion, evil lust, and covetousness, which is idolatry;
Col. 3:6 on account of which things the wrath of Elohim ^{(Mighty one(s)/God)} is coming on the sons of disobedience,
- The Law works two ways: 1) by walking in it, it will bring you life. 2) violating the law will bring destruction, and the wrath of Elohim ^{(Mighty one(s)/God)}

CHAPTER 5

Rom. 5:13 For sin was in *the* world until Law, but sin is not charged *where* there is no Law;
- **Rom. 6:23** For the wages of sin *is* death, but the gift of Elohim ^{(Mighty one(s)/God)} *is* everlasting life in Messiah Yahusha ^(replaced with Yeshua/Jesus) our Sovereign.

- **Rom. 4:15** For the Law works out wrath; for where no law is, neither *is* transgression.

- **1Joh. 3:4** Everyone practicing sin also practices lawlessness, and sin is lawlessness.

Sin causes death. Paul is saying sin was before the Law, but there is no sin without Law. So Paul is saying Law was before the (written down) Law.

Wisdom
- **Wis. 1:12** Seek not death in the error of your life: and pull not upon yourselves destruction with the works of your hands.
Wis. 1:13 For Elohim ^{(Mighty one(s)/God)} made not death: neither

133

has he pleasure in the destruction of the living.

Wis. 1:14 For he created all things, that they might have their being: and the generations of the world were healthful; and there is no poison of destruction in them, nor the kingdom of death upon the earth:

Wis. 1:15 (For righteousness is immortal:)

Wis. 1:16 But unrighteous men with their works and words called it to them: for when they thought to have it their friend, they consumed to naught and made a covenant with it because they are worthy to take part with it.

Wisdom (apocrypha)

- **Wis. 2:23** For Elohim ^{(Mighty one(s)/God)} created man to be immortal and made him to be an image of his own eternity.

  Wis. 2:24 Nevertheless through envy of the devil came death into the world: and they that do hold of his side do find it.

Rom. 5:19 For as through the one man's disobedience the many were constituted sinners, so also through the obedience of the One the many shall be constituted righteous.

What Law was added? The Law was before Mount Sinai

- **Gal. 3:15** Brothers, I speak according to man, a covenant having been ratified, even *among* mankind, no one sets aside or adds to *it*

  Gal. 3:16 But the promises were spoken to Abraham and to his Seed (it does not say, And to seeds, as of many, but as of one, "And to your Seed," which is Messiah). *Genesis 3:15; 21:12; 22:18, Rom. 9:6; Heb. 11:18*

  Gal. 3:17 And I say this, A covenant having been ratified before to Messiah by Elohim ^{(Mighty one(s)/God)}, *the* Law coming into being four hundred and thirty years after does not annul the promise, so as to abolish *it*

  Gal. 3:18 For if the inheritance *is* of Law, *it is* no more of promise; but Elohim ^{(Mighty one(s)/God)} has given *it* to Abraham through promise.

  Gal. 3:19 Why the Law then? It was for the sake of transgres-

sions, until the Seed should come, to whom it had been promised, being ordained through messengers ^(angels) in a mediator's
hand.

- **Jer. 7:21** So says Yahuah ^(Replaced with Lord/God) of Hosts the Elohim ^{(Mighty one(s)/God)} of Israel Add your burnt offerings to your
sacrifices and eat flesh.
Jer. 7:22 For I did not speak to your fathers, nor command
them in the day that I brought them out from the land of Egypt
concerning matters of burnt offerings and sacrifices.
Jer. 7:23 But I commanded them this thing, saying, Obey My
voice, and I will be your Elohim ^{(Mighty one(s)/God)}, and you shall
be My people. Also, Walk in all the ways that I have com-
manded you, so that it may be well with you.
Jer. 7:24 But they did not listen nor bow their ear. But *they*
walked in *their own* plans, in the stubbornness of their evil
heart, and went backward and not forward.

- **Amo. 5:25** Have you brought near sacrifices and food offerings
to Me forty years in the wilderness, O house of Israel?

CHAPTER 6

Rom. 6:1 What then shall we say? Shall we continue in sin that favor
may abound?
Rom. 6:2 Let it not be! We who died to sin, how shall we still live in
it?

Rom. 8:12 So, then, brothers, we are debtors, not to the flesh, to live
according to flesh,
Rom. 8:13 for if you live according to flesh, you are going to die. But
if by *the* Spirit you put to death the practices of the body, you will live.
Rom. 8:14 For as many as are led by *the* Spirit of Elohim ^{(Mighty one(s)/God)}, these are sons of Elohim ^{(Mighty one(s)/God)}.

- **Col. 3:3** For you died, & your life has been hidden with Messiah in Elohim ^{(Mighty one(s)/God)}.

- **1Pe. 2:24** who "Himself carried up in His body our sins" onto the tree; that dying to sins, we might live to righteousness, of whom "*by* His wound you were healed."

- **Gal. 2:16** knowing that a man is not justified by works of Law, but that *it is* through faith *in* Yahusha ^(replaced with Yeshua/Jesus) Messiah (we also believed into Messiah Yahusha ^(replaced with Yeshua/Jesus), that we may be justified by faith *in* Messiah and not by works of Law, because all flesh not be justified by works of Law). *Psa. 123:2*
Gal. 2:17 But if seeking to be justified in Messiah, we ourselves also were found *to be* sinners, *is* Messiah then a minister of sin? Let it not be
Gal. 2:18 For what if I build again these things which I destroyed, I confirm myself *as* a transgressor.
Gal. 2:19 For through Law I died to the Law, that I might live to Elohim ^{(Mighty one(s)/God)}.
Gal. 2:20 I have been crucified with Messiah, and I live; *yet* no longer, I but Messiah lives in me. And the *life* I now live in the flesh, I live by faith toward the Son of Elohim ^{(Mighty one(s)/God)}, the *One* loving me and giving Himself over on my behalf.
Gal. 2:21 I do not set aside the favor of Elohim ^{(Mighty one(s)/God)}; for if righteousness *is* through Law, then Messiah died without cause.

- **Matt. 16:24** Then Yahusha ^(replaced with Yeshua/Jesus) said to His disciples, If anyone desires to come after Me, let him deny himself, and let him bear his cross, and let him follow Me.
Matt. 16:25 For whoever may desire to save his life will lose it. But whoever may lose his life for My sake will find it.

- **2Co. 5:17** So that if anyone *is* in Messiah, *he* is a new creation; the old things have passed away; behold, all things have become new!

Rom. 6:6 knowing this, that our old man was crucified with *Him*, that the body of sin might be nullified, so that we no longer serve sin.
Rom. 6:7 For the *one* that died has been justified from sin.

- **2Ti. 2:11** Faithful *is* the Word: for if we died with *Him*, we also shall live with *Him*;

If we are not Under the Law, does that mean we should not keep the Commandments?

Rom. 6:14 For your **sin** shall not sovereign it over you, for you are not under Law, but under favor.

- **1Joh. 2:4** The *one* saying, I have known Him, and not keeping His commands is a liar, and the truth is not in that one.

- **Rom. 7:21** I find then the Law, *when* I desire to do the right, that evil is present with me.
  Rom. 7:22 For I delight in the Law of Elohim ^{(Mighty one(s)/God)} according to the inward man;
  Rom. 7:23 but I see another law in my members having warred against the law of my mind, and taking me captive by the law of sin being in my members.
  Rom. 7:24 O wretched man *that* I *am*! Who shall deliver me from the body of this death?
  Rom. 7:25 I thank Elohim ^{(Mighty one(s)/God)} through Yahusha ^(replaced with Yeshua/Jesus) Messiah our Sovereign! So then I myself with the mind truly serve *the* Law of Elohim ^{(Mighty one(s)/God)}, *with* the flesh *the* law of sin.

- **Rom. 8:2** For the Law of the Spirit of life in Messiah Yahusha ^(replaced with Yeshua/Jesus) set me **free from the law of sin and of death**.

- **Rom. 6:16** Do you not know that to whom you present your-selves *as* slaves for obedience, you are slaves to whom you obey, whether of sin to death, or obedience to righteousness?

- **Joh. 8:34** Yahusha ^(replaced with Yeshua/Jesus) answered them, Truly, truly, I say to you, Everyone practicing sin is a slave of sin.
  Joh. 8:35 But the slave does not remain in the house forever; the son remains to the age.
  Joh. 8:36 Therefore, if the Son sets you free, you are free in-deed.

- **2Pe. 2:18** For speaking over-swollen *words* of vanity, by *the* lusts of the flesh, by unbridled lusts, they allure those indeed escaping, the *ones* walking in error,
  2Pe. 2:19 promising to them freedom, *though* themselves being slaves of corruption; for by whom anyone has been overcome, even to this one he has been enslaved.
  2Pe. 2:20 For if by a recognition of Yahuah ^(Replaced with Lord/God) and Savior, Yahusha ^(replaced with Yeshua/Jesus) Messiah, *they* have escaped the defilements of the world, and again being entangled *they* have been overcome by these, *then their* last things have become worse *than* the first
  2Pe. 2:21 For it was better for them not to have recognized the way of righteousness than having recognized *it* to turn from the Holy commandment delivered to them.
  2Pe. 2:22 But *the* word of the true proverb has happened to them: "*The* dog turning to *his* own vomit; also, *the* washed sow to wallowing *in* mud. *Prov. 26:11*

- **1Co. 7:22** For the *one* called *while* a slave in Yahuah ^(Replaced with Lord/God) is a freed man of Yahuah ^(Replaced with Lord/God). And likewise, the *one* called *while* a free man is a slave of Messiah.
  1Co 7:23 You were redeemed with a price; do not become slaves of men.

Rom. 6:18 And having been set free from sin, you were enslaved to righteousness.
Rom. 6:19 I speak as a man on account of the weakness of your flesh. For as you presented your members *as* slaves to uncleanness and to lawless Acts unto lawless Acts, so now yield your members as slaves to righteousness unto sanctification.
Rom. 6:20 For when you were slaves of sin, you were free as to righteousness.

Rom. 6:22 But now having been set free from sin, and having been enslaved to Elohim ^{(Mighty one(s)/God)}, you have your fruit unto sanctification, and the end everlasting life.
- Set free from Sin, not the Law

CHAPTER 7

What Law is being talked about in Chapter 7. The law of Sin or the Law of Moses? In context from Chapter 6 it would be the Law of Sin. The opening of Chapter 7, speaks to those who know the Law.

Rom. 7:1 Or are you ignorant brothers, (**for I speak to those knowing Law,**) that the Law "lords" it over the man for as long a time as he lives?

- **Rom. 8:10** But if Messiah *is* in you, the body indeed *is* dead because of sin, but the Spirit *is* life because of righteousness.

Rom. 7:2 For the married woman was bound by Law to the living husband (OUR FORMER HUSBAND WAS SIN); but if the husband dies, she is set free from the Law of the husband.
Rom. 7:3 So then, *if* the husband *is* living, she will be called an adulteress if she becomes another man's. But if the husband dies, she is free from the Law, *so as for* her not to be an adulteress *by* becoming another man's.

- This is specifically dealing with the law concerning marriages, not the whole law. This teaching was only for those that know the Law (VERSE 1). Why? They understand what he was talking about. Who they were married to, SIN.

Rom. 7:4 So that, my brothers, you also were made dead to the Law through the body of Messiah, for you to become Another's, to *the One* raised from *the* dead, so that we may bear fruit to Elohim ^{(Mighty one(s)/God)}.

- **1Co. 7:39** A wife is bound by law for as long a time as her husband lives; but if her husband sleeps, she is free to be married to whomever she desires, only in Yahuah ^(Replaced with Lord/God).

- **Hos. 2:19** And I will betroth you to Me forever Yes, I will betroth you to Me in righteousness and in judgment and in mercy, and in compassions.

139

- **Eph. 5:32** The mystery is great but I speak as to Messiah and as to the assembly.

- **Isa. 54:5** For your Maker *is* your husband; Yahuah [(Replaced with Lord/God)] of Hosts *is* His name; and your Redeemer *is* the Holy One of Israel; He is called the Elohim [(Mighty one(s)/God)] of all the earth.

- **Jer. 3:14** Return, O apostate sons, declares Yahuah [(Replaced with Lord/God)]; for I am Sovereign over you. And I will take you, one from a city, and two from a family, and I will bring you to Zion.

What Law are we dead to? The Law of Sin.

Rom. 7:23 but I see another law in my members having warred against the law of my mind, and taking me captive by the law of sin being in my members.

While we are in the Flesh

Rom. 7:5 For when we were in the flesh, the passions of sin were working in our members through the Law for the bearing of fruit unto death.
Rom. 7:6 But now we have been set free from the Law, having died *to that* in which we were held, so as *for* us to serve in newness of spirit, and not *in* oldness of letter.
- **Rom. 6:1** What then shall we say? Shall we continue in sin that favor may abound?
  Rom. 6:2 Let it not be! We who died to sin, how shall we still live in it?

  Rom. 6:7 For the *one* that died has been justified from sin.

  Rom. 6:11 So also you count yourselves to be truly dead to sin, but alive to Elohim [(Mighty one(s)/God)] in Messiah Yahusha [(replaced with Yeshua/Jesus)] our Sovereign.

- **Jas. 1:15** Then having conceived lust brings forth sin. And sin being fully formed brings forth death.

Rom. 7:7 What shall we say then? *Is* the Law sin? Let it not be! But I did not know sin except through Law; for also I did not know lust except the Law said, "You shall not lust." *Ex. 20:17*
Rom. 7:8 But sin taking occasion through the commandment worked every lust in me; for apart from Law, sin *is* dead.
Rom. 7:9 And I was alive apart from Law once, but the commandment came, and sin came alive, and I died.
Rom. 7:10 And the commandment which *was* to life, this was found *to be* death to me;
Rom. 7:11 for sin taking occasion through the commandment deceived me, and through it killed *me*.
Rom. 7:12 So indeed the Law *is* Holy and the commandment Holy and just and good.
Rom. 7:13 Then that *which is* good, *has it* become death to me? Let it not be! But sin, that it might appear *to be* sin, having worked out death to me through the good, in order that sin might become excessively sinful through the commandment.

Rom. 7:14 For we know that the Law is spiritual but I am fleshly, having been sold under sin.
- **Joh. 6:63** It is the Spirit that gives life. The flesh does not profit, nothing! The Words which I speak to you are spirit and are life.

- **Rom. 8:7** because the mind of the flesh *is* enmity towards Elohim $^{(Mighty\ one(s)/God)}$; for it is not being subjected to the Law of Elohim $^{(Mighty\ one(s)/God)}$ for neither can it?

- **Psa. 51:6** Behold, You desire truth in the inward parts; and in the hidden *parts* You teach me wisdom.

- **Psa. 119:86** All Your Commands *are* faithful they persecute me *with* lying; help me!

Rom. 7:19 For what good I desire, I do not do. But the evil I do not desire, this I do.
- Gal. 5:16 But I say, Walk in *the* Spirit and you will not fulfill

the lust of *the* flesh.

Gal. 5:17 For the flesh lusts against the Spirit, and the Spirit against the flesh; and these are contrary to one another; lest whatever you may will, these things you do.

Rom 7:21 I find then the law, *when* I desire to do the right, that evil is present with me.

Rom. 7:22 For I delight in the Law of Elohim ^{(Mighty one(s)/God)} according to the inward man;

Rom. 7:23 but I see another law in my members having warred against the law of my mind, and taking me captive by the law of sin being in my members.

Rom. 7:24 O wretched man *that* I *am*! Who shall deliver me from the body of this death?

Rom. 7:25 I thank Elohim ^{(Mighty one(s)/God)} through Yahusha ^(replaced with Yeshua/Jesus) Messiah our Sovereign! So then I myself with the mind truly serve *the* Law of Elohim ^{(Mighty one(s)/God)}, *with* the flesh *the* law of sin.

- **2Co. 4:16** Because of this we do not faint but if indeed our outward man is being decayed, yet the inward *man* is being re-newed day by day.

- **Psa. 119:16** I will delight myself in Your Statutes. I will not forget Your Word.

- **Jer. 31:33** But this *shall be* the covenant that I will cut with the house of Israel: After those days, declares Yahuah ^(Replaced with Lord/God), I will put My Law in their inward parts, and I will write it on their hearts; and I will be their Elohim ^{(Mighty one(s)/God)}, and they shall be My people.

- **Eph. 3:16** that He may give you, according to the riches of His glory, by *His* power to become mighty in the inward man through His Spirit,

- **1Pe. 3:4** but the hidden man of the heart in the incorruptible *adornment* of the meek and quiet spirit, which is of great value before Elohim ^{(Mighty one(s)/God)}.

- **Col. 3:9** Do not lie to one another, having put off the old man

with his practices,
Col. 3:10 and having put on the new, having been renewed in full knowledge according to *the* image of the *One* creating him, Col. 3:11 where there is no Greek and Jew, circumcision and un-circumcision, foreigner, Scythian, slave *or* freeman, but Messiah *is* all things and in all

- **Rom. 6:16** Do you not know that to whom you present your-selves *as* slaves for obedience, you are slaves to whom you obey, whether of sin to death, or obedience to righteousness?
- **Rom. 8:7** because the mind of the flesh *is* enmity towards Elohim ^{(Mighty one(s)/God)}; for it is not being subjected to the Law of Elohim ^{(Mighty one(s)/God)}, for neither can it.
  - o What not being subject to the Law of Elohim ^{(Mighty one(s)/God)}? Flesh.

- **Rom. 8:14** For as many as are led by *the* Spirit of Elohim ^{(Mighty one(s)/God)}, these are sons of Elohim ^{(Mighty one(s)/God)}.

- **Eph. 4:23** and to be renewed in the spirit of your mind,
- Eph. 4:24 and to put on the new man, *which* according to Elohim ^{(Mighty one(s)/God)} *was* created in righteousness and true Holiness.

CHAPTER 8

What does it mean, to walk after the Spirit? (WALKING AFTER THE SPIRIT)

Rom 8:1 *There is* therefore now no condemnation to those in Messiah Yahusha ^(replaced with Yeshua/Jesus), who do not walk according to flesh, but according to Spirit.

- **2Co. 5:17** So that if anyone *is* in Messiah, *he* is a new creation; the old things have passed away; behold, all things have be-come new!

- **Gal. 2:20** I have been crucified with Messiah, and I live; *yet* no longer, I but Messiah lives in me. And the *life* I now live in the flesh, I live by faith toward the Son of Elohim ^{(Mighty one(s)/God)}, the *One* loving me and giving Himself over on my behalf.

- **1Joh. 3:2** Beloved, now we are the children of Elohim ^{(Mighty one(s)/God)}, and it was not yet revealed what we shall be. But we know that if He is revealed, we shall be like Him, because we shall see Him as He is.
1Joh. 3:3 And everyone having this hope on Him purifies himself even as that *One* is pure.
1Joh. 3:4 Everyone practicing sin also practices lawlessness, and sin is lawlessness.
1Joh. 3:5 And you know that that *One* was revealed that He might take away our sins, and sin is not in Him.
1Joh. 3:6 Everyone remaining in Him does not sin. Everyone sinning has not seen Him, nor known Him.
1Joh. 3:7 Little children, let no one lead you astray; the *one* practicing righteousness is righteous, even as that One is righteous.
1Joh. 3:8 The *one* practicing sin is of the devil, because the devil sins from *the* beginning. For this the Son of Elohim ^{(Mighty one(s)/God)} was revealed, that He might undo the works of the devil.
1Joh. 3:9 Everyone who has been begotten of Elohim ^{(Mighty one(s)/God)} does not sin, because His seed abides in him, & he is not able to sin, because he has been born of Elohim ^{(Mighty one(s)/God)}.
1Joh. 3:10 By this the children of Elohim ^{(Mighty one(s)/God)} and the children of the devil are revealed: Everyone not practicing righteousness is not of Elohim ^{(Mighty one(s)/God)}; also the *one* not loving his brother.

Rom. 8:2 For the Law of the Spirit of life in Messiah Yahusha ^(replaced with Yeshua/Jesus) set me free from the law of sin and of death.
  - Joh. 8:34 Yahusha ^(replaced with Yeshua/Jesus) answered them, Truly, truly, I say to you, Everyone practicing sin is a slave of sin.
  Joh. 8:35 But the slave does not remain in the house forever; the son remains to the age.
  Joh. 8:36 Therefore, if the Son sets you free, you are free indeed.
    o Free from what? SIN

Rom. 8:3 For the Law *being* powerless, in that it was weak through the flesh, Elohim ^{(Mighty one(s)/God)} sending His own Son in *the* likeness of sinful flesh, and **concerning sin, condemned sin in the flesh,**

- **2Co. 5:21** For He made the *One* who knew no sin *to be* sin for us, that we might become *the* righteousness of Elohim ^{(Mighty one(s)/God)} in Him.

- **Gal 3:13** Messiah redeemed us from the curse of the Law, having become a curse for us; for it has been written, "Cursed *is* everyone having been hung on a tree;" *Deut. 21:23*

- **Rom. 6:6** knowing this, that our old man was crucified with *Him*, that the body of sin might be nullified, so that we no longer serve sin.
  Rom. 6:7 For the *one* that died has been justified from sin.
  Rom. 6:8 But if we died with Messiah, we believe that also we shall live with Him,

Rom. 8:6 For the mind of the flesh *is* death, but the mind of the Spirit *is* life and peace;

- **Psa. 119:165** Great peace *is to* those who love Your Law, and there *is* no
  stumbling block to them.

- Gal. 5:18 But if you are led by *the* Spirit, you are not under Law.

Rom 8:7 because the mind of the flesh *is* enmity towards Elohim ^{(Mighty one(s)/God)}; for it is not being subjected to the Law of Elohim ^{(Mighty one(s)/God)}, for neither can it.

Who are not subjected to the Law? Servants of SIN

- **Rom. 6:20** For when you were slaves of sin, you were free as to righteousness.

Rom. 8:8 And those being in the flesh are not able to please Elohim ^{(Mighty one(s)/God)}.

- **Joh. 8:29** And the *One* who sent Me is with Me. The Father did not leave Me alone, for I do the things pleasing to Him always.

- **Joh. 15:10** If you keep My commandments you will continue in My love, as I have kept My Father's commandments and continue in His love.
  - o These are the same commandments that were taught at Mount Sinai. The Messiah was the same being at Mount Sinai. That is why He can say "My" commandments. Keep in mind, He spoke nothing of Himself, only what the Father told him, so He did.

- **Psa. 40:8** I delight to do Your will My Elohim ^{(Mighty one(s)/God)}, and Your Law *is* within My inmost *soul*

Rom. 8:9 But you are not in flesh, but in Spirit since *the* Spirit of Elohim ^{(Mighty one(s)/God)} dwells in you. But if anyone has not *the* Spirit of Messiah, this one is not His.

- **Joh. 15:5** I am the Vine; you *are* the branches. The *one* abiding in Me, and I in him, this one bears much fruit, because apart from Me you are not able to execute, nothing.

- **1Joh. 4:4** Little children, you are of Elohim ^{(Mighty one(s)/God)} and have overcome them, because He in you is greater than he in the world.

- **1Joh. 5:18** We know that everyone being generated from Elohim ^{(Mighty one(s)/God)} does not sin, but the *one* having been generated from Elohim ^{(Mighty one(s)/God)} keeps himself, and the evil *one* does not touch him.

Rom. 8:14 For as many as are led by *the* Spirit of Elohim ^{(Mighty one(s)/God)}, these are sons of Elohim ^{(Mighty one(s)/God)}.

- **1Joh. 3:1** See what manner of love the Father has given us, that we may be called children of Elohim ^{(Mighty one(s)/God)}. For this reason the world does not know us, because it did not know Him.
- **Gal. 3:22** But the Scripture locked up all under sin, that the promise by faith of Yahusha ^(replaced with Yeshua/Jesus) Messiah

might be given to the ones believing.

Gal. 3:23 But before the coming of faith, we were guarded under Law, having been locked up to the faith being about to be revealed.

Gal. 3:24 So that the Law has become a trainer of us *until* Messiah, that we might be justified by faith.

Gal. 3:25 But faith coming, we are no longer under a trainer;

Gal. 3:26 for you are all sons of Elohim ^{(Mighty one(s)/God)} through faith in Messiah Yahusha ^(replaced with Yeshua/Jesus).

Gal. 3:27 F or as many as were baptized into Messiah, you put on Messiah.

Gal. 3:28 There cannot be Jew nor Greek, there is no slave nor freeman, there is no male and female; for you are all one in Messiah Yahusha ^(replaced with Yeshua/Jesus)

Gal. 3:29 And if you *are* of Messiah, then you are a seed of Abraham, even heirs according to promise.

- **Gal. 5:18** But if you are led by *the* Spirit, you are not under Law.

Rom. 8:15 For you did not receive a spirit of slavery again to fear, but you received a Spirit of adoption by which we cry, Abba! Father!

- **1Joh. 4:18** There is no fear in love, but perfect love casts out fear, because fear has punishment and the *one* fearing has not been perfected in love.

- **Heb. 2:14** Since, then, the children have partaken of flesh and blood, in like manner He Himself also shared the same things, that through death He might cause to cease the *one* having the power of death, that is, the devil;
- Heb. 2:15 and might set these free, as many as by fear of death were subject to slavery through all the *lifetime* to live.

- **2Ti. 1:7** For Elohim ^{(Mighty one(s)/God)} did not give a spirit of cowardice to us but of power and of love and of self-control

Rom. 8:17 And if children, also heirs; truly heirs of Elohim ^{(Mighty one(s)/God)}, and joint-heirs of Messiah, if indeed we suffer together, that we may also be esteemed together.

- **Joh. 1:12** But as many as received Him, to them He gave authority to become children of Elohim ^{(Mighty one(s)/God)}, to the ones believing into His name,

- **Joh. 20:17** Yahusha ^(replaced with Yeshua/Jesus) said to her, Do not touch Me, for I have not yet ascended to My Father. But go to My brothers and say to them, I am ascending to My Father and your Father, and My Elohim ^{(Mighty one(s)/God)}, and your Elohim ^{(Mighty one(s)/God)}.

- **Heb. 2:11** For both the *One* sanctifying and the *ones* being Holy *are* all of one; for which cause He is not ashamed to call them brothers,
  Heb. 2:12 saying, "I will announce Your name to My brothers I will hymn to You in *the* midst of the assembly." *Psa. 22:22*

CHAPTER 9

Rom. 9:6 Not, however that Elohim(s) ^{(Mighty one(s)/God)} Word has failed. For not all those of Israel *are* Israel,
Rom. 9:7 nor because they are Abraham's seed *are* all children, but "In Isaac a Seed shall be called to you." *Gen. 21:12*
Rom. 9:8 That is: Not the children of flesh *are* children of Elohim ^{(Mighty one(s)/God)}, but the children of the promise *are* counted for a seed.

Paul makes reference to the Potter and the Clay. This is a Prophecy of Yahuah ^(Replaced with Lord/God) "Remaking" Israel.

Rom. 9:21 Or does not the potter have authority over the clay, out of the one lump to make one vessel to honor, and one to dishonor? *Jer. 18:6*

- **Jer. 18:2** Rise up and go down to the potter's house, and there I will cause you to hear My Words.
  Jer. 18:3 Then I went down to the potter's house, and behold, he was working a work on the wheel.
  Jer. 18:4 And the vessel that he made in clay was ruined in the hand of the potter. **So repeating he made it, another vessel** as it seemed good in the potter's eyes to make *it*.
  Jer. 18:5 And the Word of Yahuah ^(Replaced with Lord/God) was to

me, saying,

Jer. 18:6 O house of Israel can I not do to you as this potter? says Yahuah ^(Replaced with Lord/God). Behold, as the clay in the potter's hand, *so are* you in My hand, O house of Israel

- Paul was talking about Israel (That was scattered).

Paul makes reference to the Gentiles of Hosea. These are the Northern Tribes that were sent into exile.

Rom. 9:24 whom He also called, not only us, of Jews, but also out of nations.

Rom. 9:25 As also He says in Hosea, I will call those Not My people, My people! And those not beloved, Beloved! *Hosea 2:23*

Rom. 9:26 And it shall be, in the place where it was said to them, You are not My people, there they will be called, "Sons of the Living Elohim ^{(Mighty one(s)/God)}." *LXX-Hos. 2:1; MT –Hos. 2:23*

Rom. 9:27 But Isaiah cries on behalf of Israel, "If the number of the sons of Israel be as the sand of the sea, the remnant will be saved."

Rom. 9:28 For *He is* bringing *the* matter to an end, and having been cut short "in righteousness," "because Yahuah ^(Replaced with Lord/God)," "will do a thing cut short" "on the earth." *Isa. 10:22, 23*

- **Hos. 1:9** Then He said, Call his name Not My People, for you *are* not my people, and I will not be for you.

  Hos. 1:10 Yet the number of the sons of Israel shall be as the sand of the sea, which is not measured nor numbered. And it shall be, in the place where it is said to them, You *are* not My people, it shall be said to them, Sons of the Living Elohim (Mighty one(s)/God).

  Hos. 1:11 And the sons of Judah and the sons of Israel shall be gathered together, and shall set over themselves one head. And they shall go up out of the land; for great *shall be* the day of Jezreel.

- **Hos. 2:23** And I will sow her to Me in the earth. And I will have mercy on No Mercy. And I will say to Not My People, You are My people! And they shall say, My Elohim (Mighty one(s)/God)!

149

Works of the Law cannot Save you. Having Faith without works is dead. So With our Faith we must produce works. See *James 2:14-26*

Rom. 9:30 What then shall we say? That *the* nations not following after righteousness have taken on righteousness, but a righteousness of faith;

Rom. 9:31 but Israel following after a Law of righteousness did not arrive at a Law of righteousness?

Rom. 9:32 Why? Because *it was* not of faith, but as of works of Law. For they stumbled at the Stone-of-stumbling,

Rom. 9:33 as it has been written, "Behold, I place in" "Zion a Stone-of-stumbling," "and a Rock-of-offense," "and everyone believing on Him will not be shamed." *LXX and MT -Isa. 28:16; MT -Isa. 8:14*

- **Isa. 8:14** And He shall be for a sanctuary, and for a stone of stumbling, and for a rock of falling to the two houses of Israel for a trap and for a snare to the ones living in Jerusalem.

  Isa. 8:15 And many among them shall stumble and fall, and be broken, and be snared, and be taken.

  Isa. 8:16 Bind up the witness, seal the Law among My disciples.

  Isa. 8:17 And I will wait on Yahuah ^(Replaced with Lord/God), who hides His face from the house of Jacob; and I will look for Him.

  Isa. 8:18 Behold, I and the children whom Yahuah ^(Replaced with Lord/God) has given to me *are* for signs and wonders in Israel from Yahuah ^(Replaced with Lord/God) of Hosts, who dwells in Mount Zion.

  Isa. 8:19 And when they say to you, Seek to the mediums, and to spirit-knower's who peep and mutter; should not a people seek to its Elohim ^{(Mighty one(s)/God)}, *than* for the living to *seek* the *ones* who died?

  Isa. 8:20 To the Law and to the witness! If they do not speak according to this Word, *it is* because there is no dawn to them!

- **Isa. 28:16** So, Sovereign Yahuah ^(Replaced with Lord/God) says this: Behold, I place in Zion a Stone for a foundation, a tried Stone, a precious Cornerstone, a sure Foundation; he who believes shall not hasten.

- **1Pe. 2:6** Because of this it is also contained in the Scripture: "Behold," I lay in Zion" an elect "precious Stone," "a Corner-foundation;" "and the *one* believing in Him shall not be ashamed, never!" *Isa. 28:16*

  1Pe. 2:7 Then to you who believe *belongs* the preciousness. But to disobeying ones, *He is the* "Stone which those building rejected; this One became *the* Head of the Corner," *Psa. 118:22*

  1Pe. 2:8 and a Stone-of-stumbling, and a Rock-of-offense to the *ones* stumbling, being disobedient to the Word, to which they were also appointed. *Isa. 8:14*

CHAPTER 10

The "End" of the Law

Rom. 10:4 For Messiah *is* the end of Law for righteousness to everyone that believes.

- **Gal. 3:24** So that the Law has become a trainer of us *until* Messiah, that we might be justified by faith.

- **Deut. 6:25** And it shall be righteousness for us when we take heed to do all this commandment before Yahuah ^(Replaced with Lord/God) our Elohim ^{(Mighty one(s)/God)}, as He has commanded us.
  - **G5056** τελος telos *tel'-os* From a primary word τελλω tello (to *set out* for a <u>definite point or goal</u>); properly the point aimed at as a *limit*, that is, (by implication) the *conclusion* of an Acts or state (*termination* [literally, figuratively or indefinitely], *result* [immediate, ultimate or prophetic], *purpose*); specifically an *impost* or *levy* (as *paid*): - + continual, custom, end (-ing), finally, uttermost. Compare G5411.

Telos has many meanings. End or termination would put this writing out of context. Why? Because in Luke 24:44-45, the Messiah states the Law, Prophets and Psalms was written about Him. In the writings of John it states the Law of Moses writes of Him (The Messiah). Romans 10:4 is not talking about end of the law as we think today. He was showing that it was the end result, i.e. the focus or the goal of the law. Let us look at another place where this same word is used.

1Ti. 1:5 but the end of the commandment is love out of a pure heart and a good conscience, and faith not pretended,
- **Matt. 5:48** Therefore, you be **perfect** even as your Father in Heaven is **perfect**.

- **Here it is translated as perfect, not end.**

Rom. 10:5 For Moses writes *of* the righteousness *which is* of the Law: "The man doing these things shall live by them." *Lev. 18:5*
Rom. 10:6 But the righteousness of faith says this: "Do not say in your heart Who will go up into Heaven?" (that is to bring down Messiah);
Rom. 10:7 or, "Who will go down into the abyss?" (that is, to bring Messiah up from *the* dead.)
Rom. 10:8 But what does it say? "The Word is near you, in your mouth and in your heart" (that is, the Word of faith which we pro-claim) *Deut. 30:12-14.*

What is the Word of Faith? Law

Deut. 30:11 For this command which I am commanding you today *is* not too wonderful for you, nor *is* it too far off.
Deut. 30:12 It *is* not in the heavens *that you should* say, Who shall go up into the heavens for us, and bring it to us, and cause us to hear it, that we may do it?
Deut. 30:13 And it *is* not beyond the sea *that you should* say, Who shall cross over for us to the region beyond the sea and take it for us and cause us to hear it that we may do it?
Deut. 30:14 For the Word *is* very near to you, in your mouth and in your heart that you may do it

1Joh. 5:3 For this is the love of Elohim ^{(Mighty one(s)/God)}, that we keep his commandments: and his commandments are not grievous.

Rom. 10:17 Then faith *is* of hearing, and hearing through the Word of Elohim ^{(Mighty one(s)/God)}.

CHAPTER 11

Rom. 11:30 For as you then also disobeyed Elohim ^{(Mighty one(s)/God)}, but now have obtained mercy by the disobedience of these,
- **G544** α¹ειθεω apeitheo *ap-i-theh'-o* From G545; to *disbelieve* (willfully and perversely): - not believe, disobedient, obey not, unbelieving.
- Notice the connection between believing and obedience. They are linked together even in the Greek.

CHAPTER 12

Rom. 12:2 And be not conformed to this age, but be transformed by the renewing of your mind, in order to prove by you what *is* the good and pleasing and perfect will of Elohim ^{(Mighty one(s)/God)}.
- **Psa. 51:10** Create in me a clean heart, O Elohim ^{(Mighty one(s)/God)}; and renew a steadfast spirit within me.
- **Psa. 40:8** I delight to do Your will O My Elohim ^{(Mighty one(s)/God)}; and Your Law *is* within My inmost *soul*

CHAPTER 14

TALKING OF KOSHER?

Rom. 14:2 One indeed believes to eat all things, but being weak, *another* one eats vegetables.
- **2Ma. 5:27** But Judah Maccabeus with nine others or thereabout withdrew himself into the wilderness and lived in the mountains after the manner of beasts with his company, who fed on herbs continually, lest they should be partakers of the pollution.

Rom. 14:5 One-man esteems one day above another: another esteems every day *alike*. Let every man be fully persuaded in his own mind.
- **Matt. 9:14** Then the disciples of John came to Him, saying, Why do we and the Pharisees fast much, and Your disciples do not fast?

- **Luk. 18:9** And He also spoke this parable to some of those relying on themselves, that they are righteous, and despising the rest
- **Luk. 18:12** I fast twice in the week, I give tithes of all that I possess.

Tradition in the 1st century was to fast on the 2nd and 5th days.

Luk. 18:12 -
I fast twice ... - This was probably the Hebrew custom. The Pharisees are said to have fasted regularly on the second and fifth days of every week in private. This was "in addition" to the public days of fasting required in the law of Moses, and they, therefore, made more a matter of "merit" of it because it was voluntary.

Luk. 18:12 - I fast twice in the week,.... Not "on the Sabbath", as the words may be literally rendered, and as they are in the Vulgate Latin and Ethiopic versions; for the Sabbath was not a fasting, but a feasting day with the Jews; for they were obliged to eat three meals, or feasts, on a Sabbath day, one in the morning, another at evening, and another at the time of the meat offering: even the poorest man in Israel, who was maintained by alms, was obliged to keep these three feasts. It was forbidden a man to fast, until the sixth hour, on a Sabbath day; that is, till noon: wherefore, it is a great mistake in Justin and Suetonius, that the Sabbath was kept by the Jews as a fast. But the word is rightly rendered, "in the week"; the whole seven days, or week, were by the Jews commonly called the Sabbath; hence, בשבת אחד , "the first of the Sabbath", and the second of the Sabbath, and the third of the Sabbath; that is, the first, second, and third days of the week. Now the two days in the week on which they fasted were Monday and Thursday, the second and fifth days; on which days the law of Moses, and the book of Esther were read, by the order of Ezra; and fasts for the congregation were appointed on those days; and so a private person, or a single man, as in this instance, took upon him, or chose to fast on the same: the reason of this is, by some, said to be, because Moses went up to Mount Sinai on a Thursday, and came down on a Monday. But though these men fasted so often, they took care not to hurt themselves; for they allowed themselves to eat in the night till break of day. It is asked, "how long may a man eat and drink, i.e. on a fast day? until the pillar of the morning ascends (day breaks); these are the

words of "Rabbi" (Judah): R. Eliezer ben Simeon says, until cock crowing."
(Maimon. Hilch. Sabbat, c. 30. sect. 9. T. Hieros. Nedarim, fol. 40. 4. L. 36. c. 2. Octav. Aug. c. 76. Maimon. Hilch. Mechosre Caphara, c. 2. sect, 8. T. Bab. Bava Kama, fol. 82. 1. Megilla, 31. 1, 2. Maimon. Hilchot Taaniot, c. 1. sect. 5. T. Bab. Taanith, fol. 12. 1. Godwin Moses & Aaron, l. 1. c. 10. Vid. T. Bab. Sabbat, fol. 88. 1. T. Bab. Taanith, fol. 12. 1. T. Bab. Gittin, fol. 61. 1.

Matt. 9:14 Then came to him the disciples of John, saying, Why do we and the Pharisees fast often, but your disciples fast not?

Gill's Commentary on Matt. 9:24
saying, why do we, and the Pharisees, fast oft, but your disciples fast not? Not that they wanted to know the reason why they and the Pharisees fasted; that they could account for themselves, but why Messiah's disciples did not: and this is said not so
much by way of inquiry, as reproof; and their sense is; that Messiah's disciples ought to fast, as well as they and the Pharisees, and not eat, and drink, and feast in the manner they did. The fasting here referred to are not the public fasts enjoined by the law of Moses, or in any writings of the Old Testament; but private fasts, which were enjoined by John to his disciples, and by the Pharisees to theirs; or which were, according to the traditions of the elders, or of their own appointing, and which were very "often" indeed: for besides their fasting twice a week, on Monday and Thursday, Luk 18:12 they had a multitude of fasts upon divers occasions, particularly for rain. If the 17th of Marchesvan, or October, came, and there was no rain, private persons kept three days of fasting, viz. Monday, Thursday, and Monday again: and if the month of Cisleu, or November, came, and there was no rain, then the Sanhedrim appointed three fast days, which were on the same days as before, for the congregation; and if still there was no rain came, they added three more; and if yet there were none, they enjoined seven more, in all thirteen, which R. Acha and R. Barachiah kept themselves. Fasts were kept also on account of many other evils, as pestilence, famine, war, sieges, inundations, or any other calamity; sometimes for trifling things, as for dreams, that they might have good ones, or know how to interpret them, or avoid any ill omen by them; and it is almost incredible what frequent fasting some of the Rabbi's

exercised themselves with, on very insignificant occasions. They say, "R. Jose צם תמניי צומין, "fasted fourscore fasts" to see R. Chiyah Rubba; at last he saw, and his hands trembled, and his eyes grew dim: --R. Simeon Ben Lakish צם תלת מאון צומין, "fasted three hundred fasting" to see R. Chiyah Rubba, and did not
see him." Elsewhere it is said, that R. Ase fasted "thirty days" to see the same person, and saw him not. Again, R. Jonathan fasted every eve of the new year, R. Abin fasted every eve of the feast of tabernacles, R. Zeura fasted "three hundred fasts", and there are that say "nine hundred fasts".

This may serve to illustrate and prove the frequency of the Hebrew fasting. Luke represents this question as put by the Pharisees, which is here put by the disciples of John: it was doubtless put by both agreeing in this matter; and which shows
that John's disciples were instigated to it by the Pharisees, who sought to sow discord between them, and to bring Messiah and his disciples into contempt with them.
Misn. Taanith, c. 1. sect. 4. 5, 6. & c. 3. sect. 4, 5, 6, 7, 8. Maimon. & Bartenora in ib. T. Hieros. Taanlot, fol. 65. 2. & 66. 4. T. Bab. Sabbat. fol. 10. 1. Maimon Taaniot, c. 1. sect. 12-14. T. Hieros. Cilaim, fol. 32. 2. & Cetubot, fol. 35. 1. Midrash Kohelet, fol. 79. 1. lb. Nedarim, fol. 40. 4. & Taanioth, fol. 66. 1.

Barnes Commentary on Matt. 9:14
The Pharisees fasted often - regularly twice a week besides the great national days of fasting, Luk. 18:12. See the notes at Matt. 6:16-18. This was the established custom of the land, and John did not feel himself authorized to make so great a change as to dispense with it. They were desirous of knowing, therefore, why Yahusha [replaced with Yeshua/Jesus] had done it.

Rom. 14:6 The *one* minding the day, he minds *it* to Yahuah [Replaced with Lord/God]. And the *one* not minding the day, he does not mind *it* to Yahuah [Replaced with Lord/God]. The *one* eating, he eats to Yahuah [Replaced with Lord/God]; for he gives thanks to Elohim [Mighty one(s)/God]. And the *one* not eating, he does not eat to Yahuah [Replaced with Lord/God], and gives thanks to Elohim [Mighty one(s)/God].

Rom. 14:13 Then let us no longer judge one another, but rather judge this, not to put a stumbling block or an offense toward a brother.

Rom. 14:14 I know and am persuaded in Sovereign Yahusha ^(replaced with Yeshua/Jesus) that nothing by itself is common; except to the *one* deeming anything to be common, *it is* common.

Rom. 14:15 But if your brother is grieved because of *your* food, you no longer walk according to love. Do not by your food destroy that one for whom Messiah died.

Rom. 14:16 Then do not let your good be spoken evil of.

Rom. 14:17 For the kingdom of Elohim ^{(Mighty one(s)/God)} is not eating and drinking, but righteousness and peace and joy in *the* Holy Spirit.

- **1Co. 10:23** All things are lawful to me, but not all things profit. All things are lawful to me, but not all things build up.
  1Co. 10:24 Let no one seek the things of himself, but each one that of the other.
  1Co. 10:25 Eat everything being sold in a meat market examining nothing because of conscience,
  1Co. 10:26 for "the earth *is* Yahuah's, ^(Replaced with Lord/God) and the fullness of it." *Psa. 24:1*

How to Eat

Rom. 14:20 Do not by your food undo the work of Elohim ^{(Mighty one(s)/God)}. Truly, all things *are* clean, but *it is* bad to the man who eats through a stumbling block. ^(G4348)

- **G4348** ¹προσκομμα proskomma *pros'-kom-mah* From G4350; a *stub*, that is, (figuratively) *occasion of apostasy:* - offence, stumbling (-block,[-stone]).

- **Tit. 1:15** Truly, all things *are* pure to the pure, but to the ones being defiled and unbelieving, nothing *is* pure, but even their mind and conscience has been defiled.

- **1Co. 8:9** But be careful lest this authority of yours become a cause of stumbling to the weak ones. (Speaking of Food offered to idols)

- **1Ti. 4:4** Because every creature of Elohim ^{(Mighty one(s)/God)} *is* good, and nothing to be thrust away, but having been received with thanksgiving;

1Ti. 4:5 for **through Elohim(s)** ^{(Mighty one(s)/God)} **Word and supplication it is Holy**

- **You must look into the word of** Elohim ^{(Mighty one(s)/God)} to see what every creature was good to be received with thanksgiving. The Key is every creature that is GOOD. Or Clean not unclean or un-holy.

CHAPTER 15

Rom. 15:10 And again He says, "Rejoice, nations, with His people." *Deut 32:43*

- **Deut 32:43** Rejoice, O nations, of His people; for He shall avenge the blood of His servants, and shall render vengeance to His foes, and shall have mercy on His land *and* His people.

Rom. 15:18 For I will not dare to speak of anything which Messiah did not work out through me for *the* obedience of the nations in word and work,

What are we to be obedient to? The Law

Matt. 28:19 Then having gone, disciples all nations, baptizing them into the name of the Father and of the Son and of the Holy Spirit, Matt. 28:20 teaching them to observe all things, whatever I commanded you. And, behold, I am with you all the days until the completion of the age. Amen.

- What did He Command them?
- Love
- Laws and Commandments
- The Father's Will. [Which is keeping His Commandments, and Laws].

Acts 26:20 but to those first in Damascus, and Jerusalem, and to all the country of Judea, and to the nations, I proclaimed *the command* to repent and to turn to Elohim ^{(Mighty one(s)/God)}, doing works worthy of repentance.

2Co. 10:5 the demolishing of arguments and every high thing lifting up *itself* against the knowledge of Elohim ^{(Mighty one(s)/God)}, and bringing into captivity every thought into the obedience of Messiah,

2Co. 10:6 and having readiness to avenge all disobedience, whenever your obedience is fulfilled.

Heb. 5:9 and having been perfected, He came to be *the* Author of eternal salvation to all the *ones* obeying Him,

CHAPTER 16

Rom. 16:17 And brothers I exhort you to watch those making divisions and causes of stumbling contrary to the doctrine, which you learned, and turn away from them.

- **2Th. 3:6** And we enjoin you, brothers, in the name of our Sovereign Yahusha ^(replaced with Yeshua/Jesus) Messiah, to draw yourselves back from every brother walking in a disorderly way, and not according to the teaching, which you received, from us.
  2Th. 3:7 For you yourselves know how it is right to Acts like us, because we were not disorderly among you;
  2Th. 3:8 nor did we eat bread from anyone *as* a gift but by labor and toil working night and day in order not to burden anyone of you.

- **1Ti. 6:3** If anyone teaches differently, and does not consent to sound words those of our Sovereign Yahusha ^(replaced with Yeshua/Jesus) Messiah and the teaching according to righteousness,
  1Ti. 6:4 he has been puffed up, understanding nothing, but *is* sick concerning doubts and arguments, out of which comes envy, strife, evil-speaking, evil suspicions,
  1Ti. 6:5 meddling, of men whose mind has been corrupted and deprived of the truth, supposing gain to be righteousness. Withdraw from such *persons*.

- **2Joh. 1:9** Everyone transgressing and not abiding in the doctrine of Messiah does not have Elohim ^{(Mighty one(s)/God)}. The *one* abiding in the doctrine of Messiah, this one has the Father and the Son.
  2Joh. 1:10 If anyone comes to you and does not bear this doctrine, do not receive him into the house, and do not speak a greeting to him.

2Joh. 1:11 For the *one* speaking a greeting shares in his evil works.

Rumors about Paul

Acts 18:12 But Gallio *being* proconsul of Achaia, the Jews rushed against Paul with one passion and led him to the tribunal,
Acts 18:13 saying, This one persuades men to worship Elohim ^{(Mighty one(s)/God)} contrary to the Law.

Acts 21:28 crying out Men, Israelites help! This is the man who teaches all everywhere against the people and the Law and this place. And even more, *he* also brought Greeks into the temple and has defiled this Holy place.
Acts 21:29 For they had before seen Trophimus the Ephesians in the city with him, whom they supposed that Paul brought into the temple.

Acts 25:8 Defending himself, *Paul* said, Neither against the Law of the Jews, nor against the temple, nor against Caesar have I sinned in anything.

We are not to put Paul on a higher level than the rest of Scripture, he himself says this

2Co. 12:6 For if I desire to boast I will not be foolish, for I speak the truth. But **I spare, lest anyone reckons me *to be* beyond what he sees me or hears anything of me**.

1Co. 3:5 What then is Paul? And what Apollo's but ministers through whom you
believed, and to each as Yahuah ^(Replaced with Lord/God) gave?

Paul did not corrupt the Word of Elohim ^{(Mighty one(s)/God)}, which by definition of that time was the Old Testament

2Co. 4:2 But we have renounced the hidden things of shame, not walking in craftiness, **nor corrupting the Word of Elohim** ^{(Mighty one(s)/God)}, but *by* the revelation of the truth commending ourselves to every conscience of men before Elohim ^{(Mighty one(s)/God)}. Paul's letters

160

are weighty and strong

2Co. 10:10 Because, they say, the letters *are* weighty and strong, but the bodily presence *is* weak, and *his* speech being despised.
- **Weighty** (βαρειαι) In classical Greek, besides the physical sense of *heavy*, the word very generally implies something *painful* or *oppressive*. As applied to persons, *severe, stern*.
- **Weighty and strong** (*bareiai kai ischurai*). These adjectives can be uncomplimentary and mean "severe and violent" instead of "impressive and vigorous." The adjectives bear either sense.

Peter says that Paul's letters are sometimes hard to be understood because of his wisdom.

2Pe. 3:15 And account *that* the longsuffering of our Sovereign *is* salvation; even as our **beloved brother Paul** also according to the wisdom given unto him have written unto you;
2Pe. 3:16 **As also in all *his* epistles, speaking in them of these things; in which are some things hard to be understood**, which **they that are unlearned and unstable wrest**, as *they do* also the other **scriptures, unto their own destruction**.
2Pe. 3:17 You therefore, beloved, seeing you know *these things* before, **beware lest you also**, **being led away** with **the error of the wicked** (LAWLESS), fall from your own steadfastness.

Who was Paul? [Review].

1. **Paul learned from Gamaliel Acts 5:34, and was very learned Acts 22:3:**
   Therefore in order to understand the writings of Paul, we must have an understanding of the teachings of Gamaliel and Pharisees. An understanding of 1st century Teaching is needed to understand why Paul taught the things he did.

Acts 5:34 But one standing up in the Sanhedrin, a Pharisee named Gamaliel a teacher of the Law honored by all the people, commanded the apostles to be put outside a little while.

Acts 22:3 Indeed I am a man, a Jew having been born in Tarsus of

Cilicia, but having been **brought up in this city at the feet of Gamaliel, having been trained according to the exactness of the ancestral law**, being a zealous one of Elohim $^{(Mighty\ one(s)/God)}$, even as you all are today.

Acts 26:24 And he defending himself *with* these things, Festus said with a loud voice, Paul You rave **Your many letters (much learning)** turned *you* into madness.
Acts 26:25 But he said, Not to madness most excellent Festus, but I speak words of truth and sanity.

2. He was a strict Pharisee Philippians 3:5-6; Acts 26:5.

Php. 3:3 For we are the circumcision, the ones who worship by the Spirit of Elohim $^{(Mighty\ one(s)/God)}$, and who glory in Messiah Yahusha $^{(replaced\ with\ Yeshua/Jesus)}$, and who do not trust in flesh.
Php. 3:4 Even though I *might* have trust in flesh; if any other thinks to trust in flesh, I more;
Php. 3:5 in circumcision, *the* eighth day, of *the* race of Israel *the* tribe of Benjamin, a Hebrew of the Hebrews; **according to Law, a Pharisee;**
Php. 3:6 according to zeal, persecuting the assembly; according to righteousness in Law, being blameless.
Php. 3:7 But what things were gain to me, these I have counted loss because of Messiah.
Php. 3:8 But, no, rather I also count all things to be loss because of the Excellency of the knowledge of Messiah Yahusha $^{(replaced\ with\ Yeshua/Jesus)}$ my Sovereign, for whose sake I have suffered the loss of all things and count *them to be* trash, that I might gain Messiah
Php. 3:9 and be found in Him; not having my own righteousness of Law, but through the faith of Messiah, *having* the righteousness of Elohim $^{(Mighty\ one(s)/God)}$ on faith,

Acts 23:6 But knowing that the one part consisted of Sadducees, and the other of Pharisees, Paul cried out in the Sanhedrin, Men, brothers, **I am a Pharisee, a son of Pharisees;** I am being judged concerning hope and resurrection of *the* dead!
Acts 26:4 Truly, then, all the Jews know my way of life from youth, which from *the* beginning had been in my nation in Jerusalem,

162

Acts 26:5 who before knew me from the first if they will witness, that **according to the most exact sect of our religion, I lived a Pharisee**.

3. Paul taught that the Law is sound Teaching 1 Timothy 1:8-11:

1Ti. 1:8 And **we know that the Law *is* good**, if anyone uses it lawfully,

1Ti. 1:9 knowing this, that Law *is* not laid down for a righteous one, but for lawless and undisciplined ones, for unrighteous and sinful ones, for non Holy and profane ones, for slayers of fathers and slayers of mothers, for murderers,

1Ti. 1:10 for fornicators, for homosexuals, for slave-traders, for liars, for perjurers, and if any other thing opposes sound doctrine,

1Ti. 1:11 according to the good news of the glory of the blessed Elohim ^{(Mighty one(s)/God)} *with* which I was entrusted.

4. Taught the Words of Yahusha ^(replaced with Yeshua/Jesus) are Primary.

1Ti. 6:3 If any man teach otherwise, and consent not to **wholesome** ^(UNCORRUPT/TRUE) **words**, *even* the **words of our Sovereign Yahusha** ^(replaced with Yeshua/Jesus) **Messiah**, and to the doctrine which is according to righteousness;

1Ti. 6:4 He is **proud, knowing nothing**, but **doting about questions and strife's of words**, whereof comes envy, strife, railings, evil surmising,

1Ti. 6:5 Perverse disputing of men of corrupt minds, and **destitute of the truth**, supposing that gain is righteousness: from such withdraw yourself.

5. The Old Testament Is Wisdom 2 Timothy 3:15-16

2Ti. 3:15 and that from a babe you know the Holy Scriptures, those being able to make you wise to salvation through belief in Messiah Yahusha ^(replaced with Yeshua/Jesus).

2Ti. 3:16 All Scripture *is* Elohim ^{(Mighty one(s)/God)}-breathed and profitable for doctrine, for reproof, for correction, for instruction in righteousness,

2Ti. 3:17 so that the man of Elohim ^{(Mighty one(s)/God)} may be perfected, being fully furnished for every good work.

6. Believed all things The Old Testament Acts 24:14

Acts 24:14 But I confess this to you that according to the Way, which they say *is* a sect, so I worship the ancestral Elohim ^{(Mighty one(s)/God)} believing all things according to that having been written in the Law and the Prophets,

7. Called the Words of the Prophets Scripture and Law Romans 16:26 &
1 Corinthians 14:21

Rom. 16:26 but now has been made plain, and by prophetic Scriptures, according to the commandment of the everlasting Elohim ^{(Mighty one(s)/God)}, made known for obedience of faith to all the nations;

1Co. 14:21 It has been written in the Law, "By other languages" and "by other lips" "I will speak to this people," "and even so they will not hear" Me, says Yahuah ^(Replaced with Lord/God). *Isa. 28:11, 12*

8. He obeyed The Law Acts 25:8

Acts 25:8 Defending himself, Paul said, Neither against the Law of the Jews, nor against the temple, nor against Caesar have I sinned in anything.

9. He taught the Law

Rom. 10:8 But what does it say? "The Word is near you, in your mouth and in your heart" (**that is, the Word of faith which we proclaim**) *Deut. 30:12-14.*

Rom. 15:18 For I will not dare to speak of any of those things which Messiah has not wrought by me, to make the Gentiles obedient, by word and deed,

Rom. 16:26 but now has been made plain, and by prophetic Scriptures, according to the commandment of the everlasting Elohim ^{(Mighty one(s)/God)}, made known for obedience of faith to all the nations;

Eph. 5:6 Let no one deceive you with empty words, for through these *things* the wrath of Elohim ^(Mighty one(s)/God) comes on the sons of disobedience.

Eph. 5:7 Then do not become partakers with them;

Eph. 5:8 for you then were darkness, but *are* now light in Yahuah ^(Replaced with Lord/God); walk as children of light.

1Ti. 6:14 that you keep **the commandment** spotless, blameless, until the appearing of our Sovereign Yahusha ^(replaced with Yeshua/Jesus) Messiah,

Acts 21:20 And hearing, they esteemed Yahuah ^(Replaced with Lord/God), and said to him, You see, brother, how many myriads there are of Jews that have believed, and all are zealous ones of the Law.

Acts 21:21 And they were informed about you, that you teach falling away from Moses, telling all the Jews throughout the nations not to circumcise *their* children, nor to walk in the customs.

Acts 21:22 What then is it? At all events, a multitude must come together for they will hear that you have come.

Acts 21:23 Then do this, what we say to you: There are four men who have a vow on themselves;

Acts 21:24 taking these, be purified with them, and be at expense on them, that they may shave the head. And all shall know that all what they have been told about you is nothing, **but you yourself walk orderly, keeping the Law.**

10. He taught the Law is Good Romans 3:31; 7:12

Rom. 3:31 Then *is* the Law annulled through faith? Let it not be! But we establish Law.

Rom. 7:12 So indeed the Law *is* Holy and the commandment Holy and just and good.

Rom. 7:13 Then that *which is* good, *has it* become death to me? Let it not be! But sin, that it might appear *to be* sin, having worked out death to me through the good, in order that sin might become excessively sinful through the commandment.

Rom. 7:14 For we know that the Law is spiritual, but I am fleshly, having been sold under sin.

Rom. 7:22 For I delight in the Law of Elohim ^{(Mighty one(s)/God)} according to the inward man;

Rom. 7:23 but I see another Law in my members having warred against the law of my mind, and taking me captive by the law of sin being in my members.

Rom. 7:24 O wretched man *that* I *am*! Who shall deliver me from the body of this death?

Rom. 7:25 I thank Elohim ^{(Mighty one(s)/God)} through Yahusha ^(replaced with Yeshua/Jesus) Messiah our Sovereign! So then I myself with the mind truly serve *the* Law of Elohim ^{(Mighty one(s)/God)}, *with* the flesh *the* law of sin.

11. He observed the Sabbath Acts 13:42; 17:2; 18:4

Acts 13:42 But the Jews having gone out of the synagogue, the nations begged that these words be spoken to them on the next Sabbath.

Acts 13:43 And the synagogue being broken up, many of the Jews and of the devout proselytes followed Paul and Barnabas, who speaking to them persuaded them to continue in the favor of Elohim ^{(Mighty one(s)/God)}.

Acts 13:44 And in the coming Sabbath, almost all the city was gathered to hear the Word of Elohim ^{(Mighty one(s)/God)}.

Acts 17:1 And traveling through Amphipolis and Apollonia, they came to Thessalonica, where there was a synagogue of the Jews.

Acts 17:2 And according to Paul's custom, he went in to them and reasoned with them from the Scriptures on three Sabbaths,

Acts 17:3 opening and setting forth that the Messiah must have suffered, and to have risen from *the* dead, and that this is the Messiah, Yahusha ^(replaced with Yeshua/Jesus), whom I announce to you.

Acts 18:4 And he reasoned in the synagogue on every Sabbath persuading both Jews and Greeks.

12. He followed the Messiah 1 Corinthians 11:1

1Co. 11:1 Be imitators of me, as I *am* also of Messiah.

1Co. 11:2 But I praise you, brothers, that in all things you have remembered me, and even as I delivered *them* to you, you hold fast the doctrines.

- He kept the Shabbaths, Laws, and Commandments. Should we imitate him?

13. Taught from the "Old Testament"

Acts 28:22 But we think *it* fit to hear from you *as to* what you think, for truly as concerning this sect, it is known to us that it is spoken against everywhere.
Acts 28:23 And having appointed him a day, more came to him in the lodging, to whom he expounded, earnestly witnessing the kingdom of Elohim ^{(Mighty one(s)/God)} and persuading them the things concerning Yahusha ^(replaced with Yeshua/Jesus), both from the Law of Moses and the Prophets, from morning until evening.

14. He taught that we are to strive to please Yahuah ^(Replaced with Lord/God)

2Co. 5:9 Because of this, we also are striving to be pleasing to Him, whether being at home, or being away from home.

KJV 2Co. 5:9 Wherefore we labor, that whether present or absent we may be accepted of him.

15. Paul did not come teaching a new belief

2Co. 1:13 For **we do not write other things to you than what you read or even recognize**; and I hope that you will recognize even to *the* end,

16. He said to avoid contradiction of Messiah's words; 1 Tim. 6:3 and warned of false Shepherds who would come along after Him.

Acts 20:29 For I know this, that after my departing shall grievous wolves enter in among you, not sparing the flock.
Acts 20:30 Also of your own selves shall men arise, speaking perverse things, to draw away disciples after them.
Acts 20:31 Therefore watch, and remember, that by the space of three years I ceased not to warn every one night and day with tears.

17. He taught obedience

Rom. 15:18 For I will not dare to speak of any of those things which Messiah has not wrought by me, to make the Gentiles obedient, by word and deed,

Rom. 16:26 But now is made manifest, and by the scriptures of the prophets, according to the commandment of the everlasting Elohim ^{(Mighty one(s)/God)}, made known to all nations for the obedience of faith:

Eph. 5:6 Let no man deceive you with vain words: for because of these things comes the wrath of Elohim ^{(Mighty one(s)/God)} upon the children of disobedience.
Eph 5:7 Be not you therefore partakers with them.

1Ti. 6:14 that you keep **the commandment** spotless, blameless, until the appearing of our Sovereign Yahusha ^(replaced with Yeshua/Jesus) Messiah,

2Co. 10:6 and having readiness to avenge all disobedience, whenever your obedience is fulfilled.

Phm. 1:21 Trusting to your obedience, I wrote to you, knowing that you will do even beyond what I say.

2Co. 2:9 For to this end I also wrote, that I might know the proof of you, if you are **obedient** in all things.
  • **Obedient** (*hupekooi*). Old word from *hupakouo*, to give ear. In the Messianic writings only in Paul *(2Co 2:9; Phi 2:8; Acts 7:39)*.

Php. 2:8 and being found in fashion as a man, He humbled Himself, having become obedient until death, even *the* death of a cross.

Acts 7:38 This is the one who was in the congregation in the wilderness with the Angel who spoke to him in Mount Sinai and *with* our father's who received living Words to give to us
Acts 7:39 to whom our fathers did not **desire to be subject (obedient),** but thrust *him* away, and turned their hearts back to Egypt

2Co. 6:14 Do not be unequally yoked *with* unbelievers. For what partnership does **righteousness** *have* with **lawlessness**? And what fellowship does **light** *have* with **darkness**?
2Co. 6:15 And what agreement does **Messiah** *have* with **Belial**? Or what part does a believer *have* with an unbeliever?

18. He taught the Law was Holy, just and good.

Rom 7:12 Wherefore the Law *is* Holy and the commandment Holy and just and good.

1Ti. 1:8 But we know that the Law *is* good, if a man use it lawfully;
1Ti. 1:9 Knowing this, that the Law is not made for a righteous man, but for the lawless and disobedient, for the un-righteous and for sinners, for "not Holy" and profane, for murderers of fathers and murderers of mothers, for manslayers,

19. He taught the Law is Spiritual.

Rom. 7:14 For we know that the Law is spiritual: but I am carnal sold under sin.
   • He taught we should be doers of the Law.

Rom. 2:13 For not the hearers of the Law *are* just before Elohim [(Mighty one(s)/God)], but the doers of the law shall be justified.
He Taught the Commandments

1Co. 14:37 If any man think himself to be a prophet or spiritual let him acknowledge that **the things that I write unto you are the commandments of Yahuah** [(Replaced with Lord/God)].
1Co. 14:38 But if any man be ignorant, let him be ignorant.

20. He believed in keeping the Law

Acts 18:21 But bade them farewell, saying, I must by all means keep this feast that comes in Jerusalem: but I will return again unto you, if Elohim [(Mighty one(s)/God)] will. And he sailed from Ephesus.

Acts 24:14 But this I confess unto you, that after the way which they call heresy, so worship I the Elohim ^{(Mighty one(s)/God)} of my fathers, believing all things which are written in the law and in the prophets:

Acts 25:8 While he answered for himself, Neither against the law of the Jews, neither against the temple, nor yet against Caesar have I offended any thing at all

Rom. 7:25 I thank Elohim ^{(Mighty one(s)/God)} through Yahusha ^(replaced with Yeshua/Jesus) Messiah our Sovereign. So then with the mind I myself serve the law of Elohim ^{(Mighty one(s)/God)}; flesh the law of sin.

1Co. 11:2 Now I praise you, brethren, that you remember me in all things, and keep the ordinances, as I delivered *them* to you.
- *The only law that he taught against was the law of sin, and salvation through the law.*

Paul taught that he had no power against the truth

2Co. 13:8 For we cannot have any power against the truth, but on behalf of the truth.
What is truth?

21. Law & Word is Truth

Psa. 119:160 The **sum of Your Word** *is* **true**; (not necessarily verses taken out of context) every one of Your righteous judgments *endures* forever.

Psa. 119:43 And take not the **word of truth** utterly out of my mouth; for I have hoped in your judgments.
Psa. 119:44 So shall I keep your law continually forever and ever.

Psa. 119:142 Your righteousness *is* an everlasting righteousness, and your **law** *is* **the truth**.
Psa. 119:151 You *are* near, O SOVEREIGN; and all your commandments *are* truth.

Psa. 119:160 Your word *is* **true** *from* **the beginning**: and every one of your righteous judgments *endures* forever.

Mal. 2:6 The law of truth was in his mouth, and iniquity was not found in his lips: he walked with me in peace and equity, and did turn many away from iniquity.

Neh. 9:13 You came down also upon Mount Sinai, and spoke with them from heaven, and gave them right judgments, and **true laws,** good statutes and commandments:

Dan. 9:13 As *it is* written in the law of Moses, all this evil is come upon us: yet made we not our prayer before Yahuah ^(Replaced with Lord/God) our Elohim ^{(Mighty one(s)/God)}, that we might turn from our iniquities, and **understand your truth**.

Dan. 10:21 But I will show you that which is noted in **the scripture of truth**: and *there is* none that holds with me in these things, but Michael your prince.

Joh. 17:17 Holy them through your truth: **your word is truth**.

2Ti. 2:15 Study to show yourself approved unto Elohim ^{(Mighty one(s)/God)}, a workman that need not to be ashamed, rightly dividing **the word of truth.**

Joh. 8:31 Then said Yahusha ^(replaced with Yeshua/Jesus) to those Jews which believed on him, If you **continue in my word**, *then* are you my disciples indeed;
Joh. 8:32 And **you shall know the truth, and the truth shall make you free**.

22. Under Favor means stopping Sinning

Rom. 6:14 For sin shall not have dominion over you: for you are not under the law, but under favor.
Rom. 6:15 What then? **shall we sin, because we are not under the law, but under favor? Elohim** ^{(Mighty one(s)/God)} **forbid.**
Rom. 6:16 Know you not that to whom **you yield yourselves servants to obey**, his servants you are to whom you obey; whether of sin unto

171

death, or **of obedience unto righteousness?**

Rom. 6:17 But Elohim ^{(Mighty one(s)/God)} be thanked, that you were the servants of sin, but you have obeyed from the heart that form of doctrine which was delivered you.

Rom. 6:18 **Being then made free from sin, you became the servants of righteousness.**

Rom. 6:19 I speak after the manner of men because of the infirmity of your flesh: for as you have yielded your members servants to uncleanness and to iniquity unto iniquity; even so now yield your members servants to righteousness unto Holiness.

Rom. 6:20 For **when you were the servants of sin, you were free from righteousness.**

Rom. 6:21 What fruit had you then in those things whereof you are now ashamed? for the end of those things *is* death.

Rom. 6:22 But now **being made free from sin**, and become servants to Elohim ^{(Mighty one(s)/God)}, you have your fruit unto Holiness, and the end everlasting life.

Rom. 6:23 For the wages of sin *is* death; but the gift of Elohim ^{(Mighty one(s)/God)} *is* eternal life through Yahusha ^(replaced with Yeshua/Jesus) Messiah our Sovereign.

23. He delighted in the Law

Rom. 7:22 For I delight in the law of Elohim ^{(Mighty one(s)/God)} after the inward man:

Rom. 15:18 For I will not dare to speak of any of those things which Messiah has not wrought by me, to make the Gentiles obedient, by word and deed,

24. Yahusha ^(replaced with Yeshua/Jesus) is the Testator, and Him alone can change the Law.

Heb. 9:15 And for this cause he is the mediator of the ^{re}new covenant ^(testament), that by means of death, for the redemption of the transgressions *that were* under the first Covenant ^(testament), they which are called might receive the promise of eternal inheritance.

Heb. 9:16 For where a Covenant ^(testament) *is*, there must also of necessity be the death of the testator.

Heb. 9:17 For a Covenant ^(testament) *is* of force after men are dead: otherwise it is of no strength at all while the testator live.

Gal. 3:15 Brothers, I speak according to man, a covenant having been ratified, even *among* mankind, no one sets aside or adds to *it*.

25. The Good News Commonly called the "Gospel"

Some may ask why we teach new Believers to obey the Law, and its commandments. And, why not just teach the Messiah instead of the Law? Isn't that old Jewish Law done away with?
We teach Believers to obey Yahuah's ^(Replaced with Lord/God) Commandments because the Good News of Yahusha ^(replaced with Yeshua/Jesus) The Messiah itself enforces obedience to the Commandments. Second of all, what defines sin is the commandments. And thirdly, we cannot teach the Good News without teaching obedience to Yahuah's ^(Replaced with Lord/God) Law.

The Purpose for Yahusha ^(replaced with Yeshua/Jesus) Coming

Now let's consider the proof to the statements made above. Paul states,

1Tim. 1:15 This *is* a faithful saying, and worthy of all acceptation, that Messiah Yahusha ^(replaced with Yeshua/Jesus) came into the world to save sinners; of whom I am chief.

When we take the time to look from the beginning, We can see He was sent into the world for the purpose of Sin. Let's see what the angel said in Matthew.
Matt. 1:20 But while he thought on these things, behold, the angel of Yahuah ^(Replaced with Lord/God) appeared unto him in a dream, saying, Joseph, you son of David, fear not to take unto you Mary your wife: for that which is conceived in her is of the Holy Spirit
Matt. 1:21 And she shall bring forth a son, and you shall call his name Yahusha ^(replaced with Yeshua/Jesus): **for he shall save his people from their sins**.

Can you begin to see a theme here? It is all about SIN. What is SIN? Transgression of the Law. [1 John 3:4]. Let's keep going here.

Again else where Paul states, "Messiah died for our sins"

1Cor. 15:1 Moreover, brethren, I declare unto you the good news which I preached unto you, which also you have received, and wherein you stand;
1Cor. 15:2 By which also you are saved, if you keep in memory what I preached unto you, unless you have believed in vain.
1Cor. 15:3 For I delivered unto you first of all that which I also received, how that **Messiah died for our sins according to the scriptures**; (What is scripture? What is called old testament today)
1Cor. 15:4 **And that he was buried, and that he rose again the third day according to the scriptures:**

There is a lot to consider here. Paul States that Messiah died for our SIN'S, and it is written in the Scriptures. Question for you. What was scripture during their time? If you said "Old Testament" then you are correct. That was used to point out the Messiah Not Paul's letters. He states this himself.

The good news gets better. Let's read Heb.2:9

Heb. 2:9 But we see Yahusha ^(replaced with Yeshua/Jesus), who was made a little lower than the angels for the suffering of death, crowned with esteem and honor; that he by the esteem of Elohim ^{(Mighty one(s)/God)} should taste death **for every man**.

Why is this good news, Remember for the wages of sin is death. He took those sin's that was worthy of death and bore it upon Himself to save us all.

When you start to put the pieces together you should see the following.
  • He came to be the sacrificial offering for our sins.

174

And we know that sin is the breaking of Yahuah ^(Re-placed with Lord/God) Laws. Therefore, the Good News is that Yahusha ^(replaced with Yeshua/Jesus) died for our acts of breaking the Law. The Commandments of the Law, both before, and at the time of Yahusha's ^(replaced with Yeshua/Jesus) death, is what defines sin. All students of the Scriptures must admit to this fact. It is the same today *Malachi 3:6 and Heb. 13:8*.

OBEDIENCE TO WHAT WAS ONCE BROKEN (the good news)

Matt. 1:21 tells us that Yahusha ^(replaced with Yeshua/Jesus) came to save His people from their sins. We must conclude that in saving us from our acts of breaking the Commandments, Yahuah ^(Replaced with Lord/God) would require obedience to the Law that we had been breaking. He did not come to take away the Commandments that defines sin, but to take away our sins (1 John 3:5). In other words, Yahusha ^(replaced with Yeshua/Jesus) came to take away our transgressions OF the Law, but not the LAW itself, that defines our sins. Sin, transgressions, disobedience to Yahuah's ^(Replaced with Lord/God) Law commands, brought death into the world *Rom. 5:12*.

Through faith in Him and obedience to the terms of the "New Testament, we are forgiven of our sins, and at that moment, we are made free from sin, and dead to it. Then we become servants of righteousness (Rom. 6:1-2, 6, 17-18). When we are made free from sin by the power of the Set-apart Spirit dwelling within our minds and hearts, the righteousness of Yahuah's ^(Replaced with Lord/God) Law is fulfilled in us. Paul states, *"That the righteousness of the Law might be fulfilled in us, who walk not after the flesh but after the Spirit, Romans 8:4*.

The Knowledge of Sin

Paul tells us, *What shall we say, then? Is the Law sin?*

175

Elohim *(Mighty one(s)/God)* *(forbid! Nay, I had not known sin but by the Law; for I had not known lust, except the Law had said, 'You shall not covet'"* (Rom. 7:7). Paul then states, "...for by the Law is the knowledge of sin." (Rom. 3:20). Put these two statements together, and we see that Paul is definitely teaching that by the Law Commandments is the knowledge of sin for us today (and every day). He stated that he would not have known sin but by the Law, then explains further, *"For without the Law, sin is dead,"* (Rom. 7:8), and *"... for where no law is, there is no transgression," Rom. 4:15.*

In other words, Paul is saying that without the Law there is no sin. Sin, we know, is the breaking of the Law, Yahuah's *(Replaced with Lord/God)* Holy Law. And so, if Yahuah's *(Replaced with Lord/God)* Law is abolished, as some teach that it is, then there would be no sin, and if there be no sin, we would have no need for a Savior.

Attributes of the Law

Paul writes, "Wherefore the Law is Holy, and the Commandment Holy and just and good," (Rom. 7:12). If the Law and the Commandments were Holy, just and good in Paul's time, then they must still be today. So why aren't they taught today in mainstream Christianity? They do not know the Scriptural definition of what sin is.

The Law is Spiritual

Paul tells us, "For we know that the Law is Spiritual," (Rom. 7:14). Yahuah's Laws are spiritual, and only those who are spiritual, who are led by the Holy Spirit can fulfill its requirements (Rom. 8:4). If we have been cleansed and made free from sin through Yahusha's *(replaced with Yeshua/Jesus)* shed blood, and have His Spirit within us, then the righteousness of Yahuah's *(Replaced with Lord/God)* set-apart, Just and Good Law, will be fulfilled in us.

176

Perhaps you can see by now why we must teach Yahuah's ^(Replaced with Lord/God) Law when we preach the Good News of Yahusha ^(replaced with Yeshua/Jesus) the Messiah and His Kingdom. The Good News calls for us to repent, to turn away from our sins, and to accept Yahusha ^(replaced with Yeshua/Jesus) as Sovereign and Savior to save us from our sins, not to save us in our sins How can people repent of their sins when they have no idea what sin is? By the Law is the knowledge of sin, so then to know what sin is, we must study and teach Law.

Obedience to Torah or the Law

Yahusha ^(replaced with Yeshua/Jesus) preached the Good News, the same Good News that we are commanded to preach *Mark 1:14-15, 16:15-16, and Matthew 24:14; 28:19-20.*

The Sermon on the Mount is part of the Good News that Yahusha ^(replaced with Yeshua/Jesus) preached. He taught full obedience to the Commandments of Yahuah's ^(Replaced with Lord/God) Law. He commanded us to do, and to teach, all of them (Matt. 5:19). Yahusha ^(replaced with Yeshua/Jesus) did not teach a substitute law, but magnified Yahuah's ^(Replaced with Lord/God) Law *Isaiah 42:21.*

In Matt. 5:21-22, Yahusha ^(replaced with Yeshua/Jesus) magnifies the sixth Commandment to include hatred. 1 John 3:15 states, "He who hates his brother is a murderer." We must obey from the heart. If we are holding on to hatred of any kind toward anyone, we are guilty of murder, thus breaking the sixth Commandment.

In Matt. 5:27-28, Yahusha ^(replaced with Yeshua/Jesus) magnifies the seventh Commandment. He tells us that lust in the heart breaks the command that forbids adultery.
Yahusha ^(replaced with Yeshua/Jesus) the Messiah came to save us from our sins, and Yahuah's ^(Replaced with Lord/God) Law is to be written upon our hearts by the power of the Holy Spirit *Matt. 1:21; 2 Cor. 3:2,3; Heb. 8:10.*

Gal. 1:6 I marvel that you are so soon removed from him that called you into the favor of Messiah unto another good news:

Gal. 1:7 Which is not another; but there be some that trouble you, and would pervert **the good news of Messiah**.

Gal. 1:8 But though we, or a angel from heaven, preach any other good news unto you than that which we have preached unto you, let him be accursed.

Gal. 1:9 As we said before, so say I now again, If any *man* preach any other good news unto you than that you have received, let him be accursed.

Our hearts are cleansed by faith, and the love of Yahuah ^(Replaced with Lord/God) is shed abroad in our hearts by His indwelling Spirit. Lust and hatred are removed, and Yahuah's ^(Replaced with Lord/God) love compels us to total obedience to the Law commands. This is how the Good News of Yahusha ^(replaced with Yeshua/Jesus) the Messiah and the Law work together.

POINT #5. In order to prove a doctrine from the scriptures we must begin at the Law, follow though the Prophets, the writings, The Good News, and then Paul's writings. We cannot begin at Paul's writings to teach a doctrine, especially if that doctrine contradicts the rest of the Scriptures. We know that Yahusha ^(replaced with Yeshua/Jesus) is the Messiah because He fulfilled that which was written in the "Old Testament," Not because somebody wrote a letter about Him.

POINT #6 If Paul taught from the Old Testament where did He prove that the Law was done away with? If Paul was teaching believers that they need not follow the Law, What prophecy did he refer them to? Did he use "HIS LETTERS" to the Galatians as proof of his teaching? When the Breans searched the Scriptures to see if Paul was preaching the truth, did they use the "New Testament? (Keep in mind it did not exist yet). Or did they use what is called today the "Old Testament"?

1 THESSALONIANS

CHAPTER 4

1Th. 4:1 Furthermore then we beseech you, brethren, and exhort *you* by Sovereign Yahusha ^(replaced with Yeshua/Jesus), that as ye have received of us how you ought to walk and to please Elohim ^{(Mighty one(s)/God)}, *so* you would abound more and more.

1Th. 4:2 For you know what commandments we gave you by Sovereign Yahusha ^(replaced with Yeshua/Jesus).

1Th. 4:3 For this is the will of Elohim ^{(Mighty one(s)/God)}, *even* your sanctification, that you should abstain from fornication:

- **Joh. 17:17** Sanctify them **through your truth: your word is truth.**

  Joh. 17:18 As you have sent me into the world, even so have I also sent them into the world.

  Joh. 17:19 And for their sakes I sanctify myself, that they also might be Holy through the truth.

Gentiles do not know

1Th. 4:5 not in passion of lust, even as also the nations *do*, not knowing Elohim ^{(Mighty one(s)/God)};

2 THESSALONIANS

CHAPTER 1

Paul states that obedience is important

2Th. 1:8 in flaming fire giving full vengeance to those not knowing Elohim ^{(Mighty one(s)/God)}, and to those not obeying the good news of our Sovereign Yahusha ^(replaced with Yeshua/Jesus) Messiah, *Isa. 66:15; Jer. 10:25*

- **Heb. 5:9** and having been perfected, He came to be *the* Author of eternal salvation to all the *ones* obeying Him,

The great falling away

2Th. 2:3 Do not let anyone deceive you in any way, because *that Day will not come* unless first comes the falling away, and the man of sin is revealed, the son of perdition,

- The word for falling away is only used twice in the messianic writings.
  - **G646** α¹οστασια apostasia
- **Acts 21:21** And they were informed about you, that you teach **falling away** from Moses, telling all the Jews throughout the nations not to circumcise *their* children, nor to walk in the customs.

Law is in agreement with the context of Paul's letters

2Th. 2:7 For the mystery of **lawlessness** already is working, only he *is* holding back now, until it comes out of the midst.
2Th. 2:8 And then **"the Lawless One"** will be revealed, "whom" "Yahuah (Replaced with Lord/God)," "will consume" "by the spirit of His mouth," and will bring to naught by the brightness of His presence. *Isa. 11:4*

Lawlessness

- **1Joh. 3:4** Everyone practicing sin also practices lawlessness, and sin is lawlessness.

- Matt. 7:21 Not everyone who says to Me, Sovereign, Sovereign, will enter into the kingdom of Heaven, but the *ones* who do the will of My Father in Heaven.
  Matt. 7:22 Many will say to Me in that day, Sovereign, Sovereign, did we not prophesy in Your name, and in Your name cast out demons, and in Your name do many works of power?
  Matt. 7:23 And then I will declare to them, I never knew you; "depart from Me, those working **lawlessness**!" *Psa. 6:8*

Matt. 13:41 The Son of Man will send forth His angels, and they will gather out of His kingdom all the offenses, and those who practice lawlessness.

Strong Delusion

2Th. 2:11 And because of this, Elohim (Mighty one(s)/God) will send to them a working of **error** for them to believe the lie,

180

- **G4106** ¹πλανη plane *plan´-ay;* feminine of 4108 (as abstractly); objectively, fraudulence; subjectively, a straying from orthodoxy or piety: — deceit, to deceive, delusion, error.

- **2Pe. 2:18** For speaking over-swollen *words* of vanity, by *the* lusts of the flesh, by unbridled lusts, they allure those indeed escaping, the *ones* walking in error,
  2Pe. 3:17 Then beloved, you knowing beforehand, watch lest being led away by the error of the lawless you fall from *your* own steadfastness.

- **1Joh. 4:6** We are of Elohim (Mighty one(s)/God); the *one* knowing Elohim (Mighty one(s)/God) hears us Whoever is not of Elohim (Mighty one(s)/God) does not hear us From this we know spirit of truth and the spirit of error.

- **Jas. 5:20** know that the *one* turning a sinner from *the* error of his way will save *the* soul from death, and will hide a multitude of sins.

- **Eph. 4:14** so that we may no longer be infants, being blown and carried about by every wind of doctrine, in the sleight of men, in craftiness to the deceit of error,
  - o Lawlessness brings error, believing the error brings delusion, the end result will bring the spirit of error

Traditions

2Th. 3:6 And we enjoin you, brothers, in the name of our Sovereign Yahusha (replaced with Yeshua/Jesus) Messiah, to draw yourselves back from every brother walking in a **disorderly way, and not according** to the teaching tradition, which you received, from us.
- 3862. παράδοσις **paradosis,** *par-ad´-os-is;* from 3860; transmission, i.e. (concretely) a precept; specially, the Jewish traditionary law: — ordinance, tradition.

1st TIMOTHY

1Ti. 1:5 but the end of the commandment is love out of a pure heart and a good conscience, and faith not pretended,

- "end" **G5056** τελος telos same word translated end in Romans 10:4
- This is where we get the English word Telescope from. This means He is the focus of the Law in Romans 10:4. If it meant end as in it is over, then in the verse "1 Timothy 1:5", would not make since.
- **Tit. 3:9** But keep back from foolish questionings and genealogies and arguments and quarrels of law, for they are unprofitable and vain.

1Ti. 1:6 from which having missed the mark, some turned aside to empty talking (babbling),

- **Commentary from Barnes on verse 6**
  They were discourses on their pretended distinctions in the law; on their traditions and ceremonies; on their useless genealogies, and on the fabulous statements which they had appended to the law of Moses.

1Ti. 1:7 wishing to be teachers of law, neither understanding what they say, nor about that which they confidently affirm.
- **Isa. 29:13** And Yahuah (Replaced with Lord/God) says, Because this people draws near with its mouth, and they honor Me with its lip; but its heart is far from Me, and their fear of Me is taught *by* the commandments *of* men;
  Isa. 29:14 So, behold, I am adding to do wonderfully with this people, the wonder, even a wonder. For the wisdom of his wise ones shall perish, and the wit of his witty ones shall be hidden.

- Jer. 8:7 Also the stork in the heavens knows her seasons, and the turtledove and the swallow and the thrush observe the time of their coming. But My people do not know the judgment of Yahuah (Replaced with Lord/God).
  Jer. 8:8 How do you say, We *are* wise, and the Law of Yahuah (Replaced with Lord/God) *is* with us? Behold, the lying pen of the scribes has certainly worked deceit.
  Jer. 8:9 The wise are ashamed; they are terrified and are captured. Behold, they have rejected the Word of Yahuah (Replaced

182

with Lord/God), and what wisdom *is* theirs?

- **Matt. 15:14** Leave them alone. They are blind leaders of the blind; and if the blind lead the blind, both will fall into a pit

1Ti. 1:8 And we know that the Law *is* good, if anyone uses it lawfully, 1Ti. 1:9 knowing this, that Law *is* not laid down for a righteous one, but for lawless and undisciplined ones, for un-righteous and sinful ones, for un-seta part and profane ones, for slayers of fathers and slayers of mothers, for murderers,
1Ti. 1:10 for fornicators, for homosexuals, for slave-traders, for liars, for perjurers, and if any other thing opposes sound doctrine,
Was Paul saying the law was bad?

2Ti. 2:5 And also if anyone competes, he is not crowned unless he competes lawfully.

- **Neh. 9:13** And You came down on Mount Sinai and spoke with them from the heavens, and gave them right judgments and true laws, good statutes and commandments.
  Neh. 9:14 And You made Your Holy Sabbath known to them, and You commanded commandments, statutes, and laws, to them by the hand of Your servant Moses.

- **Psa. 19:7** The Law of Yahuah (Replaced with Lord/God) *is* perfect, converting the soul. The witness of Yahuah (Replaced with Lord/God) *is* sure, making the simple wise.
  Psa. 19:8 The precepts of Yahuah (Replaced with Lord/God) are right, rejoicing the heart The commands of Yahuah (Replaced with Lord/God) *are* pure, giving light to the eyes.
  Psa. 19:9 The fear of Yahuah (Replaced with Lord/God) *is* clean, endur-ing forever. The judgments of Yahuah (Replaced with Lord/God) *are* true, they are righteous altogether.
  Psa. 19:10 *They are* more precious than gold, even much fine gold, and sweeter than honey and drops from the honeycomb.
  Psa. 19:11 Also Your servant is warned by them; in keeping of them *is* great reward.

- **Rom. 7:12** So indeed the Law *is* Holy and the commandment

Holy and just and good.

- **2Pe. 1:3** As His Holy power has given to us all things *pertaining* to life and righteousness through the full knowledge of the *One* calling us through glory and virtue,
  2Pe. 1:4 by which means He has given to us the very great and precious promises, so that through these you might be partakers of *the* divine nature, escaping from the corruption in *the* world by lust.

- **Rom. 3:10** according as it has been written, "*There is* not a righteous *one*, No even one!"
  Rom 3:11 "*There is* not *one* understanding; *there is* not *one* seeking Elohim ^{(Mighty one(s)/God)} ,"
  Rom 3:12 All turned away, *they* became worthless together, not *one is* doing goodness, not so much as one!" *LXX-Psa. 13:1-3*

When one is filled with the Spirit, he doesn't "need" the law. The Spirit guides Him into all truth. Which is the Law

1Ti. 2:4 who desires **all** men to be saved and to come to a full knowledge of truth.

- **2Pe. 3:9** Yahuah ^(Replaced with Lord/God) of the promise is not slow, as some deem slowness, but is long-suffering toward us, not having purposed any to perish, but **all** to come to repentance.

- **Joh. 3:16** For Elohim ^{(Mighty one(s)/God)} so loved the world that He gave His only begotten Son, that everyone believing into Him should not perish, but have everlasting life.
  Joh. 3:17 For Elohim ^{(Mighty one(s)/God)} did not send His Son into the world that He might judge the world, but that the world might be saved through Him.

CHAPTER 4

1Ti. 4:1 But the Spirit expressly says that in latter times some will depart from the faith, cleaving to deceiving spirits and teachings of demons,

1Ti. 4:2 in lying speakers in hypocrisy, being seared in *their* own conscience,
1Ti. 4:3 forbidding to marry, *saying* to abstain from foods, which Elohim [(Mighty one(s)/God)] created for partaking with thanksgiving by the believers and *those* knowing the truth.

Those who teach that eating according to the dietary laws written in the Old Testament are no more, use this writing to say we can eat whatever we want as long as we pray over it. But looking at this writing a little closer, in verse 5, it has to be through Elohim(s) [(Mighty one(s)/God)] Word. What Word? The Word that was written in the Old Testament. He would never contradict Himself, and we know He changes not.

1Ti. 4:4 Because every creature of Elohim [(Mighty one(s)/God)] *is* good, and nothing to be thrust away, but having been received with thanksgiving;
1Ti. 4:5 for **through Elohim(s) [(Mighty one(s)/God)] Word** and supplication it is Holy

2nd TIMOTHY

CHAPTER 2

2Ti. 2:4 No one serving as a soldier entangles *himself* with the affairs of *this* life, so that he might please the *one* having enlisted *him*.
2Ti. 2:5 And also if anyone competes, he is not crowned unless he competes lawfully.
3545. **νομίμως nomimos,** *nom-im'-oce;* adverb from a derivative of 3551

- 3551. **νόμος nomos,** *nom'-os;* from a primary **νέμω nemo** (to parcel out, especially food or grazing to animals); law (through the idea of prescriptive usage), genitive case (regulation), specially, (of Moses (including the volume); also of the Gospel), or figuratively (a principle): — law.

Conclusion

After reading this book in its entirety, it is my prayer that it has shed some light on Paul's epistles. I do note that Paul's letters are inspirational and a blessing to read and understand what was taking place during his time and its particular relevance today. Keeping in mind that Paul and the twelve Apostles never had a *"New Testament,"* we know that they taught doctrine, rebuked, instructed, corrected, and proved all things from what is called the *"Old testament"* today. Paul never refers to his letters as Scripture but rather references, expounds, elaborates, and sheds light on Scripture through word of wisdom revelation inspired by the Ruach Kadesh/ Set-apart Spirit.

We should never raise Paul's writings to supersede the Scripture, especially through isogesis or surmising as we walk a dangerous path to confusion and stumbling when we attempt to infer or interpret apart from what is already there or upon what was being said. It is for this reason that said Scripture warn us against it and we do well to heed so that we avoid error. So indeed, Paul's letters are inspired and serve to enrich our lives, building up our faith in the Father Yahuah and His Son Yahusha Messiah when we have understanding.

The Messiah said that, "These are not my words, but the Father's He gave me what I should say and I know His words are EVERLASTING LIFE". (John 12:49-50). The Father would never change His Laws. He would never contradict Himself. The Messiah stated in Matthew 7:21, " Not every one that says unto me, sovereign, shall enter into the kingdom of heaven; but he that does the WILL OF MY FATHER which is in heaven". And we are not ignorant of His will for it has been revealed in Scripture.

I pray this book shed some light on the mind set of Paul and what he was up against.

Shalum,

Lamadyahu

186

Acknowledgments and dedications.

I would like to take the time to thank those that helped make this book complete. First my thanks are, above all, to our Heavenly Father and His Beloved Son that has led me to put this book together. My humble thanks to my family Abiyah and my girls. They have made many sacrifices of their time so that this book could be published. Thanks to many supporters, friends that have been vital to this work.

Key people in helping me put this book together: Medadyahu Bracey. He has helped with the editing and publication of this book. Aliyahu (Dexter) for the constant support and love to make this possible. Thanks to Yoshiyahu for his part in helping me with potential questions within Paul's letters, and his part with the editing. I like to thank Aba Kamau for her knowledge and skill sets needed in helping with editing the whole book in its final form. Also being patient with all my request and last minute add ons. Lastly the assembly for their push in motivating me to put this book together. If I missed anyone, it was not on purpose.

Made in the USA
Coppell, TX
25 February 2021